**SACRED
JOURNEY**

Mike Riddell is the author of *Godzone, Deep Stuff,
alt.spirit@metro.m3* and two novels, *The Insatiable
Moon* and *Masks & Shadows*; he also has a regular
column in the British magazine *Third Way*. He is
internationally known as a speaker and storyteller
on spiritual themes. He lives in Dunedin, New
Zealand, where he writes and lectures at the
University of Otago.

*'If you have the wisdom to see life as a journey…
Mike Riddell makes for one heck of a guide.'*
Simon Mayo

For Tomos Ffowcs Williams:
Fearless pioneer in the terrain of the spirit.
'If winter comes, can spring be far behind?'

SACRED JOURNEY

MIKE RIDDELL

Spiritual Wisdom
for Times of Transition

A LION BOOK

Copyright © 2000 Mike Riddell

The author asserts the moral right
to be identified as the author of this work

Published by
Lion Publishing plc
Sandy Lane West, Oxford, England
www.lion-publishing.co.uk
ISBN 0 7459 4425 6

First edition 2000
10 9 8 7 6 5 4 3 2 1 0

A catalogue record for this book is available
from the British Library

Typeset in 9.5/17 Book Antiqua
Printed and bound in Great Britain
by Omnia Books Ltd, Glasgow

Contents

THE SACRED JOURNEY

No snail crosses a garden path
without leaving a trail to
mark its passing; a
testament made
silver by
the light
of the sun.
And
what of you and I,
as we travel from birth to
death? Do we leave anything to
signify having navigated our way
through life? Dare we hope that it is a
journey at all, or is it an aimless wandering
lured by chance and bounded by fate? Who will observe it
with any interest, other than our mothers or those we bribe
with our affections? Is there in fact any destination at all, or
just the relentless passing of days?

By and large we suppress such disturbing
questions, filling our lives with pleasant distractions. God
knows there are enough to be had. Though perhaps in an
early morning at a lonely beach, or feeling maudlin over a
bottle of wine with a friend, or in that twilight realm before
sleep claims us, perhaps then we might allow these matters
to trouble our self-assurance. But such moments pass.

And would it have been worth it, after all,
After the cups, the marmalade, the tea,
Among the porcelain, among some talk of you and me,
Would it have been worth while,
To have bitten off the matter with a smile,
To have squeezed the universe into a ball
To roll it towards some overwhelming question…[1]

Of all the questions we will ever face, and all the challenges we are likely to encounter, surely that of the significance of our existence is the most important of them all. Why is it that so many of us only stop to ponder the meaning of our pilgrimage in times of tragedy or transition? I suspect it is because we are afraid of the answer. A pleasant obscurity may be preferable to a demanding clarity.

If there is some point to this accumulation of years which we describe as life, it may well make a difference to the way we go about the whole business. A destination implies a direction, and travelling in a certain direction entails choices, and choices require the limiting of options. By comparison, ambling along reacting to whatever falls across our path may appear a more attractive game plan.

We hide from destiny as if it were our enemy, rather than one of the most valuable discoveries we are ever likely to make. In so doing, we squander the gift of life and treat it with less respect than it deserves. The worst of mistakes is to take that which is sacred and disregard it as something trivial. It is to transgress against ourselves, and forget what is important about being alive.

 The old man was crippled and in a wheelchair. One day he went to a wedding. He talked to the bride and groom, telling them of his own wedding. He spoke of the music that had been played, the dancing that had been done. As he spoke, he began to hum one of the old tunes. He got louder and louder, and his foot began to tap to the music. Others joined in, and he burst into song. Then, before he knew what he was doing, he was out of the wheelchair and dancing before all the guests, to show them how the steps had gone. Everyone marvelled to see the crippled man dancing. And, all those years leading up to that day, he thought he'd forgotten the tune.

It's easy to forget the melody line of life. We start off well enough, with a clear idea of who we are and what we want to do. But somewhere along the way responsibilities close in on us, and we end up living blindly and without purpose. Not only have we lost the art of dancing, but we find ourselves crippled and confined to a schedule. From time to time we need to stop, remember and listen; only then does the music become audible.

I've not always been alert to life's rhythm. There have been times when I have cursed it as a punishment or sarcastic joke, days of depression and disillusionment when I was tempted to bring it to an end. At many junctures I have sought the blessed numbness of escape, whether through drugs or more subtle addictions. I recall periods of pain which I thought too intense to contain.

I was egotistical enough to imagine that I bore these wounds alone. I have subsequently learned that the one experience which binds us all as human beings is that of suffering. Pain is a reminder that we are still alive, the negative affirmation of our continuing struggle towards the light. Only now, in the second half of my life, am I willing to concede that my journey necessitates the embrace of darkness.

None of us has precisely the same path to follow, and yet all of us are summoned to follow a path. We become aware of this gravitational pull only at certain points along the way. For many of us the understanding emerges clearly in mid-life, at the very time when we suspect it is too late for us to do anything about it. Our soul knows better; it is simply time to wake up.

> Thoroughly unprepared we take the step into the afternoon of life: worse still, we take this step with the false presupposition that our truths and ideals

will serve us as hitherto. But we cannot live the afternoon of life according to the programme of life's morning; for what was great in the morning will be little at evening, and what in the morning was true will at evening have become a lie.[2]

Carl Jung claimed that the second half of life was an opportunity for spiritual growth — a season for the quest of the soul. It is that period when questions of prosperity and status are superseded by those of meaning and purpose. In some ways mid-life is a period which represents the high ground in the terrain of life; a point from which one can look both backward and forward, and gain some sense of the overall journey.

One of the greatest gifts is to become aware of life's seasons and rhythms; to distinguish spring from autumn, and to know the difference between periods of growth and periods of consolidation. Only then can we begin to be attentive to those tasks which are most important to us, instead of being seduced by the merely urgent. It is all too easy to neglect what is vital in the midst of what is demanded.

At the mid-point of life (a state which is only loosely connected to age), we have the chance to begin a period of reflection which will prepare us for our inevitable death. Or, equally, we can choose a living death by suppressing the inner voices of our soul and taking comfort in acquiring new baubles and toys to distract us. It is a period of either engagement or relinquishment, and we alone carry the responsibility for the outcome.

Many of us had strong ideals in our younger years, exciting beliefs which seemed self-evident. Life was an adventure to be lived. But somewhere along the way we lost the capacity for wonder.

 A young boy went to visit the wise old man in his castle. The man encouraged the boy to explore the castle as much as he liked.

'But while you do,' he said, 'take this.'

He handed the boy a silver spoon, on which he placed three drops of precious oil. 'This is the Essence of Meaning,' he said. 'Carry it with you wherever you go, and be careful not to spill a drop.'

The boy left on his adventure, and returned some time later.

'Well,' asked the man, 'did you like my castle? Did you see the paintings on the ceilings? What did you think of the Great Hall?'

The boy confessed that he had seen nothing of these things. He had been too busy concentrating on the spoon, and making sure that he didn't spill the oil.

'Very well, off you go again,' said the wise man. 'And this time open your eyes to that which is around you.'

When the boy returned, he had great tales of the sights which he had seen.

'But where's the precious essence which I gave you?' asked the man.

Looking down, the boy found his spoon quite empty.

'The secret of life', said the wise man, 'is to experience the wonders of life to the fullest, but to do it without losing the Essence of Meaning which you carry.'

It is possible to carry the essence of meaning without any comprehension of what it is we possess. The tragedy of our living is that we may be unaware of our loss. Neurologist Oliver Sacks tells the story of Jimmie G. — a man whose short-term memory is so damaged that he can't remember what happened even a few minutes ago. Says Sacks:

He is, as it were, isolated in a single moment of being, with a moat or lacuna of forgetting all around him… He is a man without a past (or future), stuck in a constantly changing, meaningless moment.[3]

He's not the only one. At times the whole project of Western culture seems an elaborate mechanism to delude us into forgetting our purpose, or, perhaps more accurately, into losing our way. And yet within each of us there is a voice that is not easily silenced; the deep plea of the spirit for recognition and fulfilment. We know in our hearts that our lives consist of more than what is to be seen on the surface.

Life can be diminished or demeaned; it can be impoverished or imperilled; it can be traumatised or trivialised. But one thing it can never cease to be: a gift. Even in the midst of the unspeakable horror of the concentration camp, people such as Elie Wiesel not only proclaim the worth of living but discover a new determination to embrace and uphold life.

The reality is evident to anyone with eyes to see and a heart to feel. Our existence has a depth and resonance which calls us to both celebration and discovery. There is within each of us something absolutely unique, which no other human can offer to the world. It is up to us to discover what that something is, and offer it during the course of our days. Our own souls call us to bring our gift into being.

There is a journey to be made. We are already well under way, some distance from our starting points. Unfortunately (despite the claims of many who offer them for sale), there are no precise maps available. The most we can hope for is a rough compass, the stories of fellow travellers, and the odd vantage point from which we can see the terrain ahead. Perhaps that will be sufficient.

One thing is certain; by the time we come to the end of the road, it will be too late to ponder whether we might not have paid more attention along the way. There are many forks in the path, but once we have chosen which one to follow it is very difficult to get back. Wherever you may find yourself, the answer lies in pressing forward into the unknown. We have always known that.

So let us go then, you and I, forging our way into the undiscovered territory of the mystery which constitutes our living. It is the most ancient of all human undertakings: the journey. It is the fresh scent of the breeze which beckons us on to places we know nothing of. It is the adventure we have been made for, and we will never know ourselves or others while we ignore it.

I shall be telling this with a sigh
Somewhere ages and ages hence:
Two roads diverged in a wood, and I —
I took the one less travelled by,
And that has made all the difference.[4]

BEYOND THE HORIZON

Change comes upon us. We don't go looking for it; in fact most people erect defences against it. But it finds us anyway. Sometimes change is generated by circumstances. Like a rat in a maze, we find ourselves staring at a blind alley, and realise the only viable option is to turn around and try another path.

You can lose your job, end a relationship, discover an illness, inherit a fortune, find a friend, have a baby, begin a degree or move to a new country — any of these will be sufficient to set off a process of transformation and adjustment. At least you have the satisfaction of being able to blame fate, celebrate your good fortune, curse the economy or kick the cat.

The most difficult changes, though, are those which come upon us for no obvious reason. It's possible to be trundling along, minding your own business and living life circumspectly, when all of a sudden your soul suffers a form of gastric upheaval. Feelings well up inside which are distinctly unsettling and difficult to subdue. Your dreams are troubled, your confidence is shaken and your panache is shredded. And yet all around you the world remains as it has been. The only thing which is different is your newly apparent inner turmoil. When this sort of change sneaks up on you, look out! It heralds the beginning of a process similar to white-water rafting, and equally as futile to resist.

The sad fact is that, however we may seek to protect ourselves with routines, careers or relationships, our souls have itchy feet. There is an inner force at work within even the most pedantic and regulated lives, which is intent on growth and novelty. Spiritual constipation, like its medical equivalent, is only ever a temporary state of affairs. When we go through sustained periods of conformity and lethargy, the wellspring of life within us simply builds up pressure until there is an inevitable movement of some sort. It is the illusion of static comfort we should be wary of, rather than the inevitable and entirely healthy process of change.

Do you feel the lure of the horizon? How many people in the history of humanity have looked out from some vantage point and wondered what lay beyond the perimeter of their vision? It is the unknown, the unexplored and the untasted that captivate our imaginations and call us to leave behind the familiar. It can be an impulse which leads to danger and destruction, but it is the engine of life.

Our souls are wiser than our timid reason. They grow restless in confinement, and whisper to us of wonders yet to be experienced. They are summoning us to extract ourselves from the bog of expectation and convention which mires us, and to relinquish the known for the sake of that which might yet be.

I have a golden Labrador named Baxter, who serves as both companion and spiritual director. I watch him lift his nose to the breeze, sampling whatever mysteries are carried on the air. From time to time there is something so compelling that he will dart off into the distance, literally following his nose. Sometimes it gets him into trouble. But it would be cruel indeed to restrain him and prevent him from the joy of discovery. I am trying to learn from Baxter the art of searching for that which is carried on the wind — the promise of adventures which lie beyond the horizon of the known. There is some sort of canine wisdom there which my soul recognises and delights in.

A horizon, of course, is simply the limit of what is readily apparent. We all know from experience that, given a little journeying or a new perspective, it is possible to see beyond it. What may have seemed to earlier generations the edge of the world, we have come to understand as simply the boundary of our understanding. But that which is commonplace in geography seems more tenuous when translated into spiritual topography. Surely something of the same effect applies? We live our lives within the horizons of the familiar, confident that we are in control of that territory. If events or influences intrude on that realm, it can be easier to ignore them or fear them, than to accept them as indications of life beyond the perimeter of the known. But these may be the harbingers of the adventure our souls are longing for.

Life has a way of disturbing our confident confinement within the dome of certainty. To give a name to the unnameable, God is constantly whispering in our ears of unexplored realms. At the age of nineteen I was working in a steel mill in Whyalla, South Australia. It was hot, dirty work, and one day I began to get restless and long for the road. So I put my pack on my back and began to hitch-hike north. When you're at the bottom of Australia, north is a long way to go. I travelled thousands and thousands of miles, with many adventures along the way. There were rides with mad lorry drivers, high on speed, who kept chattering and hallucinating as they drove. I picked sugar cane from the side of the road and sucked on it. Twice cars tried to run me over, presumably objecting to my long hair. A doctor picked me up in an expensive car and offered me a joint.

Eventually I washed up in Cairns, in the far north. There I found my way into a commune established in the rainforest in a place called Kuranda. It was a beautiful serene place; a site held sacred by local Aborigines. We swam naked in the pools above the Barron falls, providing an extra feature for the tourists who came past by train. Living there in quiet simplicity, I began to realise that there was more to life than was immediately obvious. In conversations around the fire at night, while fasting for short periods of time, in times of joyful dancing in the tropical rain, I began to experience the life of the spirit. The journey to Kuranda had been long, arduous and occasionally dangerous, but without it I would never have learned the mysteries which were waiting for me.

I have grown to be a watcher of skies. To the despair of would-be employers, I am constantly scanning the ether, looking for hints and signs. We can't always be on the move, of course, and travel itself can easily become as much an addiction as any other means of escape from reality. But, in certain seasons, there comes the necessity for change or growth. And I want to be alert to whatever opportunities for discovery might be presented to me. I have come to learn that I don't make this journey on my own. There is a force, a power, a being — call it what you will — that seems to be calling me on into the distance. Buried deep in the fabric of daily existence, I regularly find messages luring me to new experiences. They are rarely clear or unambiguous, but when

I am alert to them and seeking their wisdom they turn up with amazing regularity.

Not all the journeys they start me on are ones that I would choose. Some of them have been pilgrimages to the depths of my soul, where I have felt anguish sufficient to render me almost incapable of breath. All of them have led me further along the path of my discovery, however, and I do not regret them in hindsight. Nor are all the signs that have guided me gentle and benevolent. Occasionally, events have sliced through the skin of my domesticity with all the subtlety of a sharp knife. They have stabbed into my complacency with a violence and terror which causes me to recoil. Only in retrospect do I recognise their dark wisdom, and appreciate the almost brutal way in which they have recalled me to my appointed path.

When I was young my father bought a puppy which was to be our family dog. The dog grew to be boisterous and playful, but he was also a little timid. He had a particular fear of water, and refused to swim. One day my father picked the dog up and threw him off a low bridge into the middle of a small river. I was distraught and crying at such cruelty. But, lo and behold, the dog began swimming to the bank. After he had hauled himself out of the water and shaken himself dry, he leapt back into the river for another swim. After that we had trouble getting him out, and for the rest of his life he was a real water dog. I think my father knew more than the dog, and his seeming callousness was actually an act of love.

 A certain man found the pain of life to be too much for him to bear. He decided that people were untrustworthy, and that relationships led only to disappointment and heartache. So it was that he built himself a simple shelter in the woods, constructed from an old packing case. And there he took himself, furnishing it with the basic necessities of life, and living as a recluse. His life was simple, but contented. He had a bed, and a table at which to write, and even a little altar at which he prayed. The nearby lake was remote and filled with fish, and so he was able to feed himself without contact with the world.

There was only one problem for the hermit. Occasionally small rocks from the nearby mountain would dislodge and tumble down the hill, punching holes through the thin walls of his humble house. Sometimes they would hit the man on their way through, and draw blood. On one quiet night, an errant stone came through the ceiling, startling the man from his sleep, and breaking a small bone in his wrist. The man did what he could to patch the hole in his hut, and to build protective barriers to keep out the projectiles. But still they seemed to find a way around his defences.

Eventually a large boulder detached itself from the hillside and crushed the plywood house to smithereens. Luckily the man was down at the lake fishing at the time. When he returned to his shelter he was dismayed. There was nothing to be salvaged. He turned and cursed the mountain for its destructive habits. A gleam caught his eye as the sun shone on a small crevice which had been revealed by the falling rock. On investigation, he discovered a small gold nugget, and forgot his anger and frustration. Of course, it would mean a journey into town...

In the town on the other side of the mountain, an unmarried and lonely woman looked out of the window at the towering peak, and wondered what lay beyond it. The mountain remained silent.

Life does not always go as we plan — a fact for which we should be continually grateful. If it were not for interruptions to our schedules and schemes, if there were no voices calling us from beyond the horizon of the known, if things did not fall apart on us from time to time, how then would we know the work of mystery and grace which makes living beautiful? The modern concern with insurance and security is fundamentally misplaced. In our efforts to prevent anything going wrong, we may actually be confining ourselves to mediocrity — shackling ourselves with 'security chains'. Change is painful, there is no doubt. But pain is a consequence of life, and the lack of change is evidence of organisms which have ceased to be alive. No journey that is worth undertaking can be insulated from the unexpected; indeed, on the winds of the unknown come all that is worthy of pursuit.

THE ART OF LEAVING

It has been said that the secret of life is to learn how to die. Far from being a morbid preoccupation with death, this simple statement contains much wisdom. Whatever dying might mean — and there are many views on that — it is an act of leaving behind that which has been known and loved. For some it is a gracious release, for others a terrifying threat. In a life lived to full term, there is a wealth of opportunity for learning how to let go. The simple act of opening our hands to release our hold on people, places and things is at times unbearably difficult. Many people fight against it, and reach the end of their days without ever having mastered it. Like most aspects of the life fully lived, it is an art which requires application and understanding.

In youth the future seems limitless. There is always the promise of new adventures and new friends yet to come. Young people are not so concerned with departures or change, because their life stretches out in front of them like an untravelled road. However, there is a point which normally comes midway through life, when the end of the road comes into sight. At this juncture, the traveller becomes aware that some things which are lost will never be replaced. On the trivial level, these may be such cosmetic features as hair or teeth. But, more significantly, they may include highly treasured items such as dreams or friends. Goodbyes and losses then become tinged with the prospect of permanence. It marks the first awareness of the long shadow of death's inevitability.

How important it is, then, to begin early in the practice of relinquishment. There is no magic formula. Nothing takes away the pain that is a necessary part of separations, unless it is something which is used to temporarily mask the ache. As applies to so much of the soul's life, however, avoidance is not a healthy option. The way forward almost always lies through hardship rather than around it. It is unfortunate that so much of the message given by our contemporary Western societies seems to suggest otherwise. We are constantly being sold the line that success in life consists in accumulating and protecting. The art of leaving requires exactly the opposite: releasing and emptying. It is something which is best learned by navigating the experience.

A few years ago I lived in Auckland, New Zealand's

largest city. I was working full time, teaching theology to Baptist students, and doing some writing in my spare time. Rosemary, my wife, was an associate in an Auckland law firm with prospects of partnership. We had a wide group of friends, family and acquaintances, having lived in the city for some thirteen years after returning from Europe. And then it all fell apart. My first novel was published, and some of the joy of this was diminished by the fact that my Baptist employers found elements of the book objectionable. I offered to resign to save a messy process, and they readily took me up on the offer. Suddenly I faced the prospect of being unemployed. It seemed a disaster, but from early on in the process I felt a stirring in my spirit that suggested there might be more to this than simply a lost job.

Rosemary and I were in mid-life, well settled and established in our careers (or at least I was until the novel came out). We had been through some extremely difficult years as our children negotiated adolescence, and perhaps that prepared us for change. I began to wonder at the possibility of making a complete shift, of reinventing our lives entirely. I tentatively floated the suggestion that we might take the opportunity to relocate ourselves to the other end of the country. There were many benefits to be had from my perspective. We could move to Dunedin, which was a student city that had always entranced me. Housing would be cheaper, so we could afford for me to write full time. It would be a fresh start for our children. The wild landscape of Otago would be available for us to explore.

But the prospect of leaving brought into focus all that we had to lose. The fabric of our relationships would be torn, and we would be leaving people who were deep and dear friends. Many of our family members would be further away and more difficult to spend time with. In the short term, at least, our income would cease. And we would have to leave behind our lives as we had known them and constructed them. We talked with our friends and listened to their thoughts. Over a week's holiday we agonised with the decision. I watched the physical pain on Rosemary's face as she struggled with what her heart was inclined to, but every other part of her resisted. Of us all, she had the most to lose. And then, finally, we agreed to gamble on the unknown.

The idea of it was exotic and romantic; the reality slightly more sobering. I vividly remember the feeling when we climbed into our car and headed off down the southern motorway. We had sold our house behind us, and our furniture was being packed ready to be trucked to Dunedin. But we had no house there to move it into. We had manoeuvred our way through tearful goodbyes and farewells. But we had no friends or family in the city we were travelling to. We had resigned our jobs and been ceremoniously appreciated. But neither of us had work to go to in Dunedin. In short, we were leaving all that was familiar and driving towards an unknown place where we had no home, no friends and no jobs. For a fleeting moment in the car the enormity of the shift came upon me, and I felt a little sick in the stomach. We were risking an awful lot on the strength of a whim.

As it turned out, it was one of the most creative transitions in all of our married life. Our car travelled perfectly on the long drive, and promptly broke down when it reached the centre of Dunedin — perhaps making up its own mind where it wanted to stay. The day following our arrival we bought a house which was better than anything we could have imagined. We fell in love with the city and the landscape. Rosemary was hired by a law firm of which she is now a partner. Our children flourished in the new environment. With our newly attained status of being mortgage free, I was able to stay at home and write full time; a prospect I'd long dreamed of. We celebrated by getting a family dog, my aforementioned spiritual director. And spiritually, our lives exploded into a new vitality and depth.

None of it would have been possible without our willingness to bear the pain of leaving. And it was painful. Some of our dearest friends have never quite forgiven us for deserting them. I ended up walking out of projects which I and others had invested huge amounts of time and vision in, leaving my colleagues to pick up the pieces. Just recently, Rosemary's mother underwent major surgery, and we felt keenly the distance which prevented us from offering better support. And, after three years, we still have not re-established anything like the networks of support which we had in our previous setting. There has been pain — but no regret. The time had come when it was right for us to re-engage with the project of life, and to do so demanded we pay the cost of letting go of much which was precious.

Not all shifts need to be geographic ones, of course; nor is it always necessary to undergo such a dramatic upheaval in order to overcome the lethargy of mid-life. We had become moribund, locked in pack ice and unable to move. The only hope of escape for us necessarily involved a great deal of shattering and turmoil. But at any stage of life, and in any circumstances, growth and journey will entail some leaving. When we open our eyes to the world we can see that no organism matures without giving up something which was previously precious. Empty nests, dry seed husks and vacated cocoons all speak to us in silent testimony of the cost of growth.

Some elements of the art of leaving have become apparent to me over time, and I share them for what they are worth. The first and most fundamental is an abiding confidence in the goodness and purpose of life. Without this we will fight against what we imagine to be arbitrary and random intrusions on our peaceful comfort. In order to go with the currents of life and not resist them, we need to have great trust in the process. Secondly, we need to understand that anything which is within our hearts cannot be taken away by external forces. We retain the power to hold onto or let go of that which we love. Saying goodbye is a voluntary act of relinquishment.

Thirdly, we must learn the lesson that seeds must die in order for plants to grow. In other words, our dreams and visions cannot be reached without the surrender of what previously contained them. Jesus, who I stubbornly believe abides as a source of truth despite what the church has done to rebury him, had this to say of his own fate and of life in general:

> Unless a grain of wheat falls into the earth and dies, it remains just a single grain; but if it dies, it bears much fruit.

He went on to say that those who are set on holding on to their life and preserving it end up losing it altogether, whereas those who are ready to risk losing it gain more than they could hope for.

Fourthly, how we make our goodbyes is of supreme importance. We need to take the time to do them properly. The temptation to avoid pain by hasty escape is misplaced. We have to exchange the words of love, remembrance and regret with the people we are being separated from. And often it is helpful to create some ritual of leaving. At the time our family was deciding to move to Dunedin we were together for New Year's Eve. Over the day, we began a process of making lists: one a list of all that had gone wrong for us in life and what we wanted to abandon, the other a list of our personal visions of the future. Late in the evening, we sat in a circle and read out those parts of the lists we were willing to share with the others, and talked about them. Just before midnight, we burned the lists which contained our regrets, to symbolise the fact we were putting them behind us. I still have the little container which holds those ashes. This simple family ritual helped enable us to make a major transition.

Fifthly, we should be aware that there is a gap between letting go of the old and the arrival of the new. It is the terrible gap of unknowing; the dark space where the familiar is out of reach and the nascent is not quite visible. It is the time between letting go of the rope and discovering whether there are friendly arms to catch you. In such periods we may feel that all is lost and slip into despair. We long for our former securities and mourn their passing. This much is normal and to be expected. But some people become desperately afraid at such junctures. They seek to make their way back to what has gone, or else they become so full of self-pity and regret that they are blinded to the birth of the new when it comes. Times of transition are times of danger, and it is important to learn how to navigate them safely.

It is only when we reach the far shores of major change that we can look back and see some of the distance we have travelled, and perhaps become dimly aware of why that particular part of our journey was necessary. This is knowledge which it is impossible to have in advance, and only those who are willing to take the utter risk of leaving will experience the joy of discovery. We are all of us trapeze artists; to get from one side to the other we have to be willing to let go of the trapeze we are holding, and hang for a few moments in suspended animation before we grasp the next support on our wild ride into the unknown.

FACING THE UNKNOWN

Most people are fearful of the unknown, and for good reason. Facing genuinely new experiences means that our previous wisdoms and resources are often made redundant. Dealing with such fresh encounters forces us to reach beyond our conditioned responses. We have to respond to new realities in real time, adjusting our reactions and judgments on the wing. It is both frightening and exhilarating. Fear of the unknown has driven many people into a lifelong attempt to defend against it. They construct such a range of protections around their existence that their souls suffocate in the stale air of certainty. On the other hand, some become addicted to the adrenalin rush of newness, and spare no effort in disrupting any temporary harmony they might experience for the sake of novelty.

Something in between is both possible and more productive. If we are to grow into all that we have been created to be, then we will be continually confronting situations which are at least partially unknown. But if we are to build upon our learnings rather than simply amusing ourselves with a kaleidoscope of experiences, then there will be a need to stop and consolidate from time to time. The journey of life is often pieced together from phases of rapid growth and discovery, followed by more settled periods of integration. Trees should not be planted indoors, nor should seedlings be uprooted every few days to see if they are growing.

One of the most magic journeys I ever made was a train trip through Spain, from Madrid to Algeciras. I was on my way to Morocco, following the well-worn hippy trail. We wound our way through steep mountain passes, where peasants with donkeys wandered amid the olive groves. Eventually I arrived in Algeciras, and spent some time waiting for the ferry across the Mediterranean to North Africa. I stopped in a coffee shop and got talking to a fellow traveller. He was on his way back from Morocco. He had not had a happy time there, and advised me not to go. It would be foolhardy, he told me, and recounted stories of tragedy and disaster to back up his warning. I listened carefully and respectfully, and then I went anyway.

Not long afterwards, I found myself in a Moroccan prison, charged with possession of hashish. I spent some six weeks there, in the most miserable conditions I have ever experienced. Every day was a battle against violence, disease and despair. I don't regret having ignored the warning, however. I needed to go and find out for myself, needed to test myself against unexplored territory. I learned things in prison I could never have learned any other way, and some of those lessons inform me still. For my journey in that time, the unknown produced the substance of what most of us would consider our worst fears. And yet they were fears I needed to confront and survive through. No one else could have done that on my behalf.

 The story is told of an adventurer who set out from a small village on an island in the Pacific Ocean. He paddled his solitary canoe over the horizon, and was not seen again for more than twenty years. His family had given up on him, long considering him dead. Then one day he startled them all by returning. His face was lined and dark with age, and his eyes deep and penetrating. After the welcoming feast, he sat with the other villagers around the fire and recounted some of the adventures of his travels. He spoke of far lands where people lived in high towers and wore clothes which covered most of their bodies. He told of great mountain ranges and lands so big that the sea could not be seen from even their highest point. He described the way he had navigated by the stars

to find his way back to the island again.

The villagers were greatly excited, and wanted to hear his stories again and again. When he grew tired of entertaining them, they insisted that he draw them a map of the lands he had visited and the way to get there. This map was mounted on a pole in the centre of the village, and became the object of a great deal of veneration. The people learned the names of the various towns depicted on it, and took pride in being able to explain how to navigate to the far places. Some of the older ones began to tell the stories of certain places as if they themselves had been the ones who had seen them. But one thing the villagers never did: they never took the risk of crossing the wide seas for themselves, to learn if the stories were true.

The unknown is the realm of possibility. In the known world everything is fixed and certain. Freedom requires the prospect of novelty; without it there can be no genuine freedom. Surely that is why we resist the notion of a blind and fixed fate. We know that it confines us to conformity and the tyranny of the fixed order. Our souls know, even if we do not, that we humans are born to freedom. Only in freedom do we become who we are. It is the element in which we are truly at home. Deprived of it we are like fish out of water, flopping uncertainly in a slow gyration of death.

Creativity also demands a universe which is open to new possibilities. Artists are people who see something which does not yet exist, and then spend their lives trying to create it. And all of us are artists, if we will let ourselves become so. In that strange territory of the unknown lie all our hopes and aspirations. If the land is closed to us through our own disbelief or fear, we are destined to be perpetually frustrated. If, on the other hand, we can find the courage to become explorers ourselves, then the realm of the new will become for us a place of wonder and deep satisfaction. The enemy of spiritual discovery remains our own timidity and concern for safety.

What resources are there to strengthen us inwardly for the journey into the unknown? One of the most important is to have a framework which can help us to make sense of things we have not previously encountered. Obviously, we must first have a world-view which allows for the unexpected and regards it without fear. While that may seem basic, it is amazing how many people there are who live in such a way as to deny surprise. When something out of the ordinary occurs, they either deny that it happened at all, or else they see it as confirmation of an already existing belief. At one time I thought that no one could sustain such a way of life for any great length of time. But experience has taught me that stubborn resistance allows some people to bunker down and live their entire allotment of days in reliance on beliefs they gained quite early in life.

But, for those who are prepared to face the adventure of the soul's journey, there needs to be some means of relating what is new to what has gone before. If the new entirely obliterates the past, then it becomes a destructive force which will destroy human continuity and peace. Many of the world's traditions of wisdom, however, both allow for the new and teach us to be continually alert to its presence. The Way of Christ, for example, by which I live, is not a closed perspective but an open one. It suggests a continuous surging creative drive at work in the world, which is relentlessly transforming life. It prepares me for hope, for loss, for change, for suffering, for grace, for surprise and for wonder. When it seems to me that God is acting in new ways in my life, I don't have to dispense entirely with my former experience, but can allow it to be renewed and enriched.

Another resource might be that of the community of our friends. When we encounter the unknown, we often need help to determine whether it greets us as friend or foe. Our souls know, even if our minds sometimes disregard the message, that there is a difference between good and evil. All travellers know that a path must be picked carefully if one is to survive the journey. When we are perplexed because we're going through experiences we've never faced before, it is often helpful to seek the counsel of people we trust. It is not necessary that they are wiser or more experienced than us, merely that they love us.

When Rosemary and I faced the prospect of leaving Auckland on the journey south described in the previous chapter, we consulted our friends. They were certainly not disinterested. We like to think that their natural instincts were to preserve our friendship by retaining us in the same city. But they loved us enough to try to think and pray with us in our exploration of a radical shift. Slowly and reluctantly they agreed that they sensed what we did — it was time to move. It was a great gift to us, born out of their own pain. It didn't guarantee success, but it did give us a great deal of confidence as we set out on the road to an unknown future.

It sometimes helps in greeting the new to adopt an attitude of travelling lightly. This becomes harder to do materially the older we get. We easily become weighed down with a multitude of possessions and commitments. When that's the case, then there is a lot to lose in any drastic change of direction. By degrees, we gain a stake in the status quo, and become people who are defensive rather than passionate. When it comes to that final journey at the end of our earthly days, there is little we can take with us except what has found its way to our hearts. From time to time it helps to recall that, and loosen our ties to things we own or the obligations we feel. No one is indispensable; when an object is lifted out of water, the water closes behind it and there is little evidence of its passing.

An important aspect of entering unfamiliar territory is a commitment to hold your course in the face of obstacles. Once you've let go of the old for the sake of the new, there can be no turning back. Many years ago, when our children were younger, we were driving down a shingle road out in the backblocks. It was a dark and moonless night, and I was driving fast and at the limit of the headlights. We came around a bend, and there in front of us was a single lane bridge with concrete walls on either side.

It was getting cold, and I reached down with one hand to switch the heater on. As it happened, I flicked the wrong switch and our headlights died. Instantly we were hurtling along in impenetrable darkness. There was no time to fiddle for the light switch. I was aware that the narrow bridge was rapidly approaching, but I could see nothing. My only option was to stay with what I had seen of the bridge in the light, and hold my course. Somehow we made it across to the other side. My heart was beating wildly, but I had learned a lesson about keeping to your path once you've started on it.

The unknown need not fill us with dread. Understood properly, it can be welcomed and embraced as an essential part of spiritual growth. It is, like my misadventure on the bridge, a journey into the darkness. But after some years of experience, we begin to learn to trust the process, and to go with it rather than fight against it. In doing so, the darkness leads us to the light.

HINTS
OF
GOD

Perhaps the most concise and easily accessible religious confession was coined anonymously sometime in the twentieth century: shit happens. It represents a point of almost universal consensus regarding human existence. Unfortunately, few of us are willing to leave it at that. We want to know why, how, and maybe even who. I think it's fair to say that everyone who has ever lived life at depth has some awareness of something going on — a force, a current, a spirit or whatever. A tide, if you want to use Shakespearean terms. People involved in twelve-step recovery programmes speak about it as their Higher Power.

Does this force have a name? Is it arbitrary or purposeful? Can it be plugged into, or is it as remote as a magnetic field? These are questions which can be fruitless highbrow intellectual preoccupations, or can be part of a heartfelt quest to drive to the core of reality. They awaken the soul and enliven the spirit. Whichever way we come at it, it is the big G question, and everyone has their own answer. People sensibly duck for cover in the presence of religious propagandists. But, if you take the time to ask, almost everyone has some experience of a big Something which has impinged on their life from time to time. A friend of mine named it Umbra Major (the great shadow) in order to talk about it without preconceptions.

I might as well come clean and admit to my own belief in and tangled relationship with God. Other people might argue whether God exists or not; I've never been allowed that luxury. Somehow I've always had an awareness of Someone looking over my shoulder. Which doesn't mean to say that I am naive or have any forelock-tugging predilection to servitude. From time to time I curse God or demand explanations. All I am saying is that I can't imagine that I'm shouting my questions into an empty and unresponsive void. My experience of living prevents me from either atheism or agnosticism, as attractive as they might seem at times. Forgive me if I take the reality of God for granted; it's not an attempt to claim the high ground, but an impediment along the lines of a crippled leg.

One of the good things about God is subtlety. God is not in your face all the time, which is why people can get by without acknowledging there's Anyone out there. It's a kind of relaxed, take-it-or-leave-it attitude which, unfortunately, is not shared by that multitude of people who act as self-appointed agents to God. I appreciate God's subtlety; it shows panache, and leaves me a lot of space to make choices. It does mean, however, that the divine presence is never obvious. If you want to find it, you have to search. You need to become a prospector of the spirit; an explorer beyond the boundaries of the mundane.

What we have in life and the world is nothing more than hints of God. These are as ephemeral as wisps of blue smoke highlighted in a stray beam of sunlight. Always ambiguous, these delicate hints are something akin to the fragrance of God's presence. Once you have come to know that scent, your senses become keen to it and you are for ever sampling the air to check for it. But if you don't recognise it, you can continue about your business completely oblivious. I don't think anyone was ever convinced about God by argument. The only path to knowing God is to have your eyes opened to Someone who has always been there.

This entire journey of the soul of which we speak is grounded in the life of God. Our restlessness, our hunger for understanding, our dissatisfaction with the world as it is; our sense of purpose and direction, our intimations of significance, our awareness of being lured beyond the horizon; these all begin to make sense once we understand that our lives are not arbitrary or meaningless. There is a call forward in all of our lives. What is it towards? Or, to phrase it slightly more helpfully, Who is it towards? God is the ultimate secret of living, and the source of life itself. We journey because God is a traveller; we love because God is a lover; we dream because God is an artist.

Once our eyes are opened, the world is full of God. We see it so easily in the glories of nature: in tranquil pools amid tree-covered peaks; in the silence of the dawn as the sun haunts the early sky; in the heaving seas as they connect with something in the depths of our souls. But God is also to be found in less likely places: around the meal tables in hostels for psychiatric patients; in the shining eyes of an old woman as she allows a memory to touch the surface of her mind; in the quiet and contented babbling of a baby. Those who are blind to divinity will see nothing other than what is obvious, while those who are enlightened will be overwhelmed by mystery and meaning.

I once attended an exhibition in which there was a room that was entirely dark. When I entered it from the bright light of outside I could see nothing at all. If I had been in a hurry I might have moved straight out again, convinced that there had been nothing to see. But I waited for a while, and, as my eyes slowly became adapted to the darkness, works of art emerged. They had been there all along, of course, but I had not been ready to see them. I suspect something similar is necessary in order to see the handiwork of God. We need to stop occasionally and wait — to linger in the journey through life so that the eyes of our soul may readjust from the dazzling lights of commerce and consumption.

To see is to know that God is love, and that life is good. No one will ever believe this who does not experience it for themselves. Love is indescribable. It is perhaps the strongest force which rakes the human spirit, and yet it is entirely invisible. To the scientific observer, it might be classified as a minor neurosis; to the beloved, it is a foretaste of heaven. Love and God are not the same thing, but wherever love is, you can be sure God is not far away — and vice versa. When we learn for a certainty that God is love and that life is good, we understand the essence of existence, and our pilgrimage is made both simpler and infinitely more joyful.

The best story I know about God is the one sometimes called 'The Prodigal Son'. It is undoubtedly a Christian story, told by Jesus, but is no less profound for either that or for its familiarity. The story is a simple one. It concerns a son working on the family farm, who grows restless. He talks to his father about getting his inheritance early, so that he might strike out on an adventure. The father agrees, and the son leaves with his share of the family legacy in his pocket. He travels to a far land, where he begins to live the fine life with his father's money. Naturally he has many friends, attracted by his generous lifestyle. But eventually the money runs out. He has to look for work, and ends up as a hired hand on a pig farm.

One day, while feeding the slops to the pigs, he begins to think of all he has lost by leaving home. Even the servants on his father's farm are well fed, and treated with respect. And so he decides to take the long road back. Along the way, he concocts the story he will use to get back into his father's good graces, and perhaps gain a job as a labourer. But, in the end, he never gets to use it. While he is still toiling his way up the hill to the family home, his father, who has been watching out the window, comes running down the road to greet him. He falls upon his wayward son and embraces him. Then he takes him inside, dresses him in fine clothes, and begins preparations for a great welcoming feast. 'For my son who was dead to me is alive,' he says, 'and the one who was lost has come home.'

It is a story about God and a story about us. About us, in that we are the ones who are continually wanting to cash up our lives; we want to extract as much as we can from our days on earth, and use it to put some distance between ourselves and the fount of our existence. We search out the far lands of ecstasy and nirvana — through drugs, through sex, through luxury, through fame, through religion or through self-indulgence. The story is also about us, in that even when, in quiet moments, we become aware of our loneliness or lack of satisfaction, we are apprehensive about finding the road home. We fear the kind of reception we might receive, and are full of self-justifying excuses to explain our profligate behaviour.

But, more importantly, it is a story about God. About God, firstly, in that God never stands in the way of our desperation to flee our place of belonging. If we demand to extract our due, then it is given to us. God not only allows but encourages our journey into freedom. We are free to go as far as we like, and live however we choose. What then does God do? God waits; waits and watches. Sits in the window, hoping for our return. And if the beloved face should be glimpsed, God will rush out to greet us and draw us in for a celebration. This is not the God of punishment, nor the God of hellfire-and-brimstone enthusiasts. It is the God of love; the God who forgets all wrongs in the fire of compassion. That is what God is like.

There is much in our own experience to suggest otherwise. We find ourselves rejected, abandoned, abused, betrayed and hurting. The fine lives we have imagined for ourselves in our youth fail to eventuate, and we feel resentful towards whatever cosmic force might be guiding our lives.

Pain is easily corroded into bitterness and resentment. Surely, if there is a God, that being is using divine power against us rather than for us. The ephemeral nature of God in our hour of need suggests that we are encountering just another absent father, who delights in withholding love and inflicting punishment. Nothing could be further from the truth. The Christian story is quite the opposite — it is we who inflict pain on God our Lover and the good gift of creation.

The best way to experience the reality of God is to become completely empty, and then to explore what lies beyond such emptiness. This is why those who have been hollowed out by suffering are often the first to discover God. Most times we resist both pain and emptiness, going to great lengths to gain comfort for our wounds and distraction from the inner void. For those who find the grace to journey beyond desolation, there is the encounter with what might best be described as liquid love: pure, endless, undemanding, all-consuming love. Having touched the hem of God's garment once, there is no need for further words, qualifications or explanations. Love is its own argument, and those who touch it even briefly carry that experience in their souls for evermore.

Shit happens. And in the midst of the shit, God. In surprising places, amid inexcusable circumstances, in the presence of raw pain, beneath the deepest anguish, within the simplest joy, there is God the companion, quietly awaiting recognition. This our souls already know, if we will allow them to speak.

ROAD SIGNS

Any intentional journey has a departure point and a destination. But between those two points there is an almost infinite range of options as to how the distance might be traversed. It is no different for the journey of the soul. Our choices are legion; often so much so that they paralyse the cautious traveller into inaction. Picking a path is the task of life — the adventurous interplay between the voice of God, which calls us forward, and our own exercise of freedom as we find our unique way. Travel contains challenges and dangers, however. It can be every bit as threatening as it is exciting. On the journey of the spirit, it is wise to heed the signs which former travellers have left behind to help those who follow. Such road signs give vital information for our own pilgrimage.

Reduce Speed

It is a condition of contemporary life that all of us seem to be in a hurry to get wherever it is we are going. But when the path we follow leads us through risky terrain, it may be necessary to slow down a little in order to navigate the hazards safely. When you have been travelling at speed, of course, slowing down seems so unnatural as to be almost physically painful. There comes an instinctive rebellion against the loss of forward momentum. On New Zealand roads, signs indicating the need to reduce speed constitute one type of warning to travellers. The other sort, which is probably more convincing, is provided by small white crosses at periodic intervals to mark the sites where drivers have crashed and died. Slow progress may be better than its alternative.

Reducing speed in life requires a conscious decision. Various elements which contribute to the breakneck pace of existence need to be relinquished — at least temporarily, and possibly permanently. Some people have such limitations forced upon them by the experience of stroke, heart attack or cancer. Their bodies become virtual neon signs, warning them of the consequences of continuing to live at an unsustainable tempo. But the rest of us need to be alert to subtle indications that a particular period of our journey demands the respect of slowing down. We have to be willing to give up on the dream of being omnicompetent, reducing some of the breadth of our lives for the sake of achieving depth in selected areas. In simple terms, this means giving up some things we find both enjoyable and worthwhile.

I find it necessary about once every three months to review my various commitments. They accumulate over time, like the accretion of barnacles on the bottom of a boat. Various employers of mine have found this intensely frustrating, as I am regularly seeking to vary the terms of my employment according to my circumstances in life, often in a downward direction. At one time I considered myself invulnerable — every new task was a challenge to prove myself capable of it. Too late I discovered that I had become hollow inside, and that I was losing touch with my children, for whom 'quality time' became a euphemism for very little time. Only gradually did I find the courage to give up on some spheres of activity. Three things happened in consequence: nobody missed my contributions; I became better at the things that remained; and I began to remember what it meant to be a soulful human again.

No Stopping

In contrast, there are stretches of highway where it is simply unwise to stop at all, and the best course of action is to keep moving. Sometimes in life it is sensible to go with the flow, and not try to resist by planting your feet firmly in the ground. We've all met people who have stopped at a certain point of their development, and who resolutely refuse to travel any further. You can recognise them by the putrid smell of decay, as their souls decompose within them. There is a variety of causes for such premature stagnation, from bad experiences to good ones. Some people, when they suffer great pain, either physical or emotional, respond by fixating on their hurt and loss so that it becomes the enduring centre of their existence. They encase it in a cocoon of bitterness, and then proceed to feed upon it for the remainder of their lives.

Others have some high point of experience, which might be generated by a religious encounter, a drug high, or even simply the vigour and freedom of youth. This retrospective peak then becomes the measure of everything subsequent, a standard to which nothing ever quite attains. They, therefore, spend all of their days seeking to recreate that initial experience, growing in frustration and desperation as they discover that it is unrepeatable. These people, too, have become stuck in their journeys, and are so concerned with living out of the past that they sacrifice any ongoing present. Experiences are essentially ephemeral — they are best taken neat and savoured for what they have to teach. But we can no more hold onto them than we can bottle the wind. The attempt to do so cripples and immobilises us.

A traveller was crossing a vast sweep of desert-like terrain. In the distance she spied a small dwelling. It was remarkable in being the only sign of human habitation in an otherwise empty landscape. Eventually the pilgrim arrived at the house and, out of curiosity, knocked on the door. A weary man answered. He invited her in. Inside she discovered it was decorated as a sort of shrine. And the centre point of devotion was a photo of an attractive woman. The man explained that this was a picture of his beloved, who had become lost in the wilderness and died on this very spot. He recounted many stories of her, and then, looking intently at his visitor with renewed interest, remarked how much she resembled his lost love.

'I have to move on,' said the woman. 'Why don't you come with me?'

But the man looked at her with great sadness in his eyes.

'How could I?' he asked. 'It would mean leaving all this behind.'

And so he bid goodbye to the woman he had been mourning for most of his life.

Major Intersection

If there were only one path to follow in the course of our travels, then life would be a great deal simpler than it is. But we are faced with a multitude of roads, each beckoning us onto its untravelled surface. Many of them are alternative routes for reaching the same destination, but some are sidetracks or even dead ends. From time to time we approach major intersections, where the choices we make about which road to follow will be binding and irrevocable. These are places of crisis and decision, from which the overall direction of our lives is constructed. When we reach them, these intersections require that we pause and consider the options that are open to us, rather than simply rushing through them.

Life is valuable enough to be worthy of reflection as to its purpose. It's no good getting to the end of the journey and looking back regretting that the events of daily routine have carried us along. Where we end up will naturally enough be influenced by the circumstances we've encountered along the way. But in equal part it will also be determined by the choices we make. Crossroads are places of great opportunity, and are sacred for that reason. At each one we face the prospect of choosing for or against the vital life of the soul; for or against the quiet voice which calls us towards what may well be the more difficult path. Care is the most we can bring to bear in these moments; certainty is beyond our reach. As Thomas Merton has expressed in prayer, confusion should not be regarded as limiting:

My Lord God, I have no idea where I am going.
I do not see the road ahead of me.

I cannot know for certain where it will end.

Nor do I really know myself,

and the fact that I think I am following your will

does not mean that I am actually doing so.

But I believe that the desire to please you

does, in fact, please you.

And I hope I have that desire in all that I am doing.

I hope that I will never do anything apart from that desire.

And I know that if I do this

you will lead me by the right road,

though I may know nothing about it.

Therefore, I will trust you always though I may seem

to be lost and in the shadow of death.

I will not fear, for you are ever with me,

and you will never leave me to face my perils alone.[5]

No U-Turns

Going back is never a good idea in the spiritual life. Even with the most difficult of experiences, the secret is to move into them rather than to retreat from them. If in a moment of weakness we back off from the difficult, it is not unusual for us to be stunted in our growth until we arrive back at the same point and overcome our fears. There is a biblical story told of the people of Israel after they have fled Egypt. They travel through the desert until they come up against the border of a new land. The people make camp there, and Moses organises for a group of spies to go into the new territory to check it out. When they come back, they have conflicting reports.

The majority opinion is that, while the land is rich and fertile, it is inhabited by people so large and strong that to enter it would be suicidal. A couple of the others agree that it is dangerous, but suggest that the dangers are worth it for the rewards to be reaped. They describe it as the promised land, and urge the people to cross the border. After a great deal of grumbling and many expressions of fear, the assembled multitude decides to take the soft option, and to turn back. It is the beginning of their forty years' wandering in the wilderness; a time which only comes to an end when they return to that very same frontier and find the courage to cross it. They are fortunate to be given a second chance to make good their earlier failure of nerve.

There is an awareness in the depths of our souls that not much which is valuable is easily won. Pressing on in times of uncertainty and deep pain is commonly the right response, if not always the easy one. We must learn to navigate our way through the small losses, disappointments and deaths, so that when the big ones come we are partly prepared for them. Turning back, or escape in any form, is generally avoidance of that which is ultimately inescapable.

And for those who do seek to return to that which they
have left, there is the discovery that it has gone, never to be
retrieved in quite the way they knew it. Upward and onward
is the best course for the soul, with a deep trust that even
when shadows fall over the valley, the path will open out
into light again somewhere further along.

Give Way

From time to time, travellers' paths intersect, and there is
meeting or confrontation. There may be conflicting directions
and contradictory stories concerning the best road to be
followed. Those who are sure of their way are often keen to
convince others to join them. But beyond the mind and will's
predilection for conversion, there is the gentler wisdom of
the soul which counsels deference to the stranger. To give
way in simple humility is to surrender nothing other than
arrogance, and allows for both discovery and encounter. The
heart of love is forgiveness; that ability to lay down one's
own rights and agendas for the sake of the other. Against
such there can be no argument.

 *A certain woman knew herself to be dying, and so set out on
a journey to discover the meaning of life. It turned out to be a
long and adventurous trip. One day she met another woman
coming towards her on the path.*

'Where are you headed?' she asked this stranger.

'I'm on a pilgrimage to find the meaning of life,' replied the woman.

'Then we are heading for the same destination. But we are travelling in opposite directions.'

'One of us must be travelling the wrong way.'

'Perhaps,' said the dying woman. 'On the other hand, each of us knows and has come from the place that the other is heading towards. Why not share our stories?'

The two women talked long into the night. It happened that the older one breathed her last that very evening, and died in the arms of her new friend. In the morning, the lone pilgrim continued her journey into the unknown. She had learned that even when two people are travelling in opposite directions, it does not necessarily mean that one is going the wrong way.

TRAVELLING COMPANIONS

No life comes into being in
isolation. The mystery of
the universe is such
that our formation
requires the
active
participation
of others. From
the very beginning,
the legacy of our genes
bears witness to our essential
dependence on the braided
tributaries of the life which is passed
on to us. We cannot escape from the fact that
we are the product of human community, and that our lives
are intimately bound up with others who travel a similar
journey to our own. Nor, in the best of worlds, should we
want to. It is a bizarre development in the tide of history that
we have become so isolated from one another that we regard
our self-contained separation with a certain amount of pride.
Those who can function without significant support from
others are described as independent and self-reliant, while
the desire for relationship is treated as evidence of some
weakness.

In the life of the soul, there are some journeys to be

made and tasks to be achieved which can only be undertaken alone. But always the healthy soul is integrated into a social and communal fabric, apart from which existence becomes distorted. In short, we do not travel the paths of the spirit alone, and those who attempt to do so can almost guarantee tragedy. From the early days of human history, travellers have recognised the benefits of banding together for a time, and particularly of gathering to share stories and wisdom gleaned from experiences along the way. Friendship, intimacy, trust, generosity, belonging; these and many other qualities can only be learned in the company of travelling companions.

We only learn our true identity when our lives are lived in concert with fellow nomads. In the furnace of relationship we begin to discover where we end and the other person begins. We recognise what it is that we have to give which is different from anything anyone else can offer. We learn something of what our journey means from the gentle observations of our friends. We find what it means to engage our individual will with the wisdom of the group. We name and are named; we love and are loved. It is one of those delightful paradoxes — we can only fully discover who we are as individuals in the context of community.

But it is not always easy to accept the needs of

friends, neighbours or lovers. Even young babies squall when they find that their own desires must be fitted into the needs of parents or siblings. The rubbing up against one another of people produces all sorts of things, the most common of which is pain. Each person is simultaneously limited and fulfilled by participation in a group. People, after all, are primarily annoying; and most especially those people who are closest to us. They interfere, they demand, they disappoint, they transgress, they advise, and − horror of horrors − they do things differently from how we would have done them. Small wonder that strong-minded folk are loath to have their lives complicated by friends.

The value of community only arises when the social veneer has been penetrated, and the real and painful differences between people become depressingly obvious. If everyone were the same and agreed on all points, achieving community would be both easy and pointless. As it is, we have to learn the valuable spiritual lesson of accommodation in order to maintain relationships. That is to say, we must recognise and then make room for the differences which manifest themselves in every life. We learn the art of making space and time within our hearts for someone who is clearly 'not-us', and thereby extend the hospitality of the soul. This is an essential ingredient of the capacity for love;

without such hospitality our relationships become a form of narcissism.

One of the keys to spiritual growth is to look on each new person we encounter along the way as someone who has been sent to us with a gift. They have some lesson to teach us, some quality to awaken in us, some blessing to bestow on us, some need for us to fulfil or some question to ask of us. When we regard people this way we cease to look on even the apparently most obnoxious as enemies, and rather begin to probe for their essential mystery. It is astonishing how such a simple change of orientation towards people can release grace and discovery for those willing to try it. But first we must learn to overcome our own prejudice and fear.

The story is told of a set of twins who grew up together in an ancient village in Latvia. One day some militiamen came through the town. They required a boy to look after their horses, and, spying a young lad playing in the fields, seized him and rode off with him. The boy's twin brother was left alone in the village, and over the years was consumed with grief at the loss of his constant companion. Nothing was ever heard of the hostage, but when his twin grew to be a man, he heard a rumour that his brother had been sighted in a far-off town. He immediately gathered provisions and set off on the long journey.

Eventually he reached the militia town, but before he could even begin searching for his brother he was taken by the border sentries and thrown into jail as a spy. There he was treated roughly, and interrogated daily by a brute of a man who beat him and refused to believe the story of the lost twin. The prisoner grew to dread his torturer, and spent all his spare time plotting revenge. Every bruise and welt he received served to increase his hatred for the man. One day his jailer came to him subdued, and said he would release him. When asked what had happened, he explained that his favourite horse had just been shot, and he didn't have the stomach for torture anymore.

The prisoner saw the deep grief in the man's eyes, and for a fleeting moment his hatred faltered and was replaced with sympathy. And in that instant he saw what he had been blind to all of the time — his jailer and tormentor was none other than the brother he loved and had lost. For a long while afterwards, they cried together. And then they embraced.

Everyone has a story to tell, and, once we have heard it, it becomes impossible to demonise them ever again. Forgiveness is often simpler than it seems; it only requires that we spend sufficient time with our enemies to learn that they are the same as us. We are capable of all the good and all the evil that has ever been done, and this recognition is the beginning of grace. Once we know it, we can stop looking for heroes to save us, or villains to punish, and accept that in our own hearts lies the genesis of that which we both condemn and praise. When those who travel with us have been freed of our expectations and judgments they become available to us in all of their intriguing distinctiveness. In our own liberty, we are enabled to both listen and learn, without feeling the need to interject, convert or qualify.

Friendship is the greatest of all forms of love, because it is the love of equals. Often couples are drawn to each other for a variety of not-so-pure reasons, including codependency and lust. Their early years are frequently marked by power struggles, in which one or the other seeks to gain control, or to make their partner into someone lovable. Only when this has been relinquished are they able to discover the warmth of genuine friendship, where love is purified of any agenda other than enjoyment and companionship. When Jesus tells his followers that they are no longer to be regarded as disciples but as friends, it is the highest honour he might bestow on them. Any hierarchy or religious formality has been subsumed in love.

Loneliness is one of the cruellest conditions that anyone can suffer. The absence of touch, the lack of laughter and the absence of someone to hear our stories is a crippling indignity. This unsought isolation must be distinguished from solitude, which is the periodic choice to enter into a deep and refreshing silence for the sake of stilling other voices. Though the only difference may be in whether the experience is sought or imposed, that difference is monumental in its effects. All people need intimacy as the connecting thread in the weave of their existence, and it is a tragic commentary on our times that so many find it unavailable, or have to resort to rather sad imitations of it.

Companions save us from delusion, and can be instrumental in helping us to find the way forward. Within the sacred trust of friendship, it is possible for people to speak honestly and perceptively with one another, and without it taking on the character of criticism. This is the only way many of the deepest and most secret issues in our lives can be addressed without causing damage. In the presence of our friends, we are able to be truly ourselves without need for pretence or apology. We can reveal the ugly sides of our personalities, secure in the knowledge that we won't be rejected because of them. This is a great help in allowing the dark side of the soul to be recognised and integrated, rather than suppressing it whereupon it inevitably wreaks havoc.

Of course, the love of others opens us to the possibility of betrayal and heartache. That is a necessary consequence of deep friendship — it is impossible to love without becoming radically vulnerable. And people, being what they are, often disappoint each other; sometimes irrevocably so. As the old saying has it: 'Better to have loved and lost, than never to have loved at all.' Love requires openness to pain, or else it is something less than love. When people like me say that God is love, then at least one of the things we mean by it is that God has become exposed to whatever suffering we as the beloved may inflict through our betrayal and desertion. We in turn are susceptible to the sense of abandonment and lack of intervention which we may feel we have received from God.

God, for those who have some awareness of the divine, is the ultimate travelling companion. Here we find One who is constantly with us in all the adventures and mistakes of our journey. The wisdom of the soul is to know God, and to perceive hints of that searching presence beyond the surface events of life. In cultivating the sense of divine friendship, we are able to enter any situation without hunger for affirmation or fear of recrimination. We find ourselves already deeply befriended, and so are excused any unbalanced frenzy for acceptance or valuing by the people we encounter along the way. And the great cosmic secret is that God is, and always has been, a traveller at heart; pressing on restlessly towards some unknown horizon in search of yet another adventure. This may be why our souls are equally restive as they reach out for fulfilment.

WAITING...

Patience is not only a virtue, but an attitude to life which can be achieved solely through attention to the inner journey. I have to confess that I am not one to whom patience comes naturally. Rather than waiting quietly for doors to open, my instinct is to race forward and tear them off their hinges to see what lies behind them. The problem with patience is that there's no quick way to learn it. In fact it is one of those lifelong projects that is only finally validated by our demeanour in the final days of our earthly existence. I have been slowly and incrementally learning that all my desperation to lay hold of the future does little except devalue the present. Serenity is merely the outward face of a soul which is content to be still in the face of the world.

Many years ago I was at a rock concert in Greenwich, London, somewhat the worse for wear. Most of the crowd were using mind-altering substances of one kind or another. It was an excellent concert, but my partner and I decided to leave a little before the finish of the last act in order to avoid the crowds. Making our way to the exit, we found ourselves amid a group of about a hundred people, all pressed up against a locked gate. Some were pounding against the gate; others were jabbering with a touch of paranoia about why the police had shut us all in the stadium; a few were wailing in fear. The situation was perplexing, until I spied an open gate some thirty metres to the left, with a large 'Exit' sign in full view. Here people were walking out freely and without impediment. I've sometimes wondered if there are still a few hippies banging on that closed gate.

Our attitude to life can sometimes be akin to that exhibited by the anxious mob. We push up against obstacles, demanding to be allowed past, when a little time and observation might allow us to find a better path to follow. Waiting is a form of humility, while pressing forward exerts our selfishness and arrogance. The restlessness of our souls is not helped by the fact that we live in a society where waiting is regarded as at best an unnecessary imposition and at worst a violation of human rights. We have become accustomed to instant responses of various kinds, and now we demand them. Sometimes the very worst thing happens, and we get what we have demanded, to our eternal regret.

Perhaps it is because in our newly urban sphere of

life we have begun to lose touch with the idea of seasons and maturity. In earlier times, when lives were integrally related to the rhythms of the earth, it may have been more obvious that growth can never be rushed without the loss of something important. Crops must be allowed to grow to maturity, and there is no point in either harvesting them early or bemoaning their slow progress. Ripening is an entirely natural process, and, at the right time, our period of waiting and nurturing is rewarded. The growing cycles are themselves dependent on the slow wheel of the seasons, to bring them the conditions which will foster their development. Farmers may watch the skies closely, but they have learned that they must work in harmony with larger forces if they are to bring in a rich harvest.

The spiritual life is not all that much different. There are also times and seasons in the progress of the soul, and we do well to work in cooperation with them rather than fighting against them. There are qualities and dreams being formed within us which might suffer serious damage if plucked too early. They require a safe environment of gestation; a quiet space where growth is allowed and protected. One of the gifts of wisdom is the ability to recognise ripeness and the seasons. Too soon and we taste the sourness of our impatience; too late and the anticipated fruit has already begun to perish. It is a useful practice to take regular stock of what is happening in the inner life so that, when the time for harvest comes, we recognise it.

Many things which are good in life take a considerable amount of time. Those who drink red wine will be aware of the marvellous complexities which develop in it over the long years of rest in a wine cellar. I greatly admire those people who are able to gain a perspective on their life's work, and who often don't achieve their unique accomplishments until they have served an apprenticeship of some thirty or forty years. Nelson Mandela proved to be a man of vision, courage and humility. Over the period of his captivity in prison, he underwent the process of preparation. For many it was unimaginable that he should emerge as a national leader, and revolutionise the face of South Africa. But, when his time came, he was ready with the attributes of reconciliation, forgiveness and generosity. He was a man in season.

The learning of patience is agonising. It requires that we let go of so many things we wish to control. There is a difference, however, between patience and passivity. Passivity is a fatalistic attitude that has been forced on people by the weight of circumstance, and under the sway of which they feel powerless to effect any change on the world. Patience, on the other hand, is something that is chosen; it is an active and intentional waiting which grows from an attitude of trust towards the essential goodness of life. It is a craft which must be learned through practice. It seems to me that every time I learn to extend my patience a little further, some new event will come along which stretches me just that bit more than I am prepared to go. I suspect that is the only way to develop patience — similar to athletes who incrementally increase their performances.

The mysterious dance of our lives is a partnership between our free creativity and the incessant magnetic lure of the divine. Like any dance, it requires a certain amount of grace to carry it off. Certainly, we have absolute liberty to choose our own steps, and those who are determined to can construct their entire existence in a kind of rigorous solo performance. But when our own moves are designed in concert with the prompts and urges of our cosmic dancing partner, then we become the people we hoped to be. To do so requires attentiveness to quiet nudges of spirit; an openness and receptivity to our distinctive cues in life. We need to learn to be alert to the hints and signs which emerge from daily existence, and which hold the potential to be navigational beacons on our journey into the unknown.

Rushing headlong at the future may not always be the best method of picking a path. When lost in the dark, it is not a bad idea to sit absolutely still for some time and listen, straining to pick up any clues which might help. Similarly, on the sacred journey of life, our souls have the ability to recognise the ambiguous pointers God scatters amid the cobblestones, but they need to be allowed the space in which to do it. Attentiveness is an approach to life which waits carefully and peacefully, secure in the knowledge that nothing is lost by giving respect to the importance of finding the right way. It demands that we learn the discipline of pausing to reflect, rather than riding impulsively into the distance.

Waiting is not only a form of prayer, it is the essence of prayer. It is a form of self-emptying, in which we forswear our own desires and ambitions for the sake of listening for Another. Many people have gained the idea that prayer is about asking, and some turn it into a form of demanding to have their own way. Nothing could be further from the truth — prayer is a means of entering the womb of silence in order to hear what lies beyond words. It is a way of waiting on God; the sort of prayer a farmer makes as he sits on his veranda and quietly watches the sun shining on the wheat. He knows two things: nothing he can do will make the wheat grow, and his watching of the wheat is nevertheless a part of its growth.

 A Catholic man lived a life of humble poverty. Every day he prayed to Mary that she would take pity on him and grant him a life of wealth and comfort. In the early years of his prayer, he

was confident that she would grant his desire. Each day he
was faithful to repeat his request. After many years of prayer,
however, the man began to change his priorities. He became less
interested in gaining wealth and comfort, and more conscious
of learning to love. He began to give the little he had away to
the poor, and eventually retreated to the woods where he lived
a life of subsistence and prayer. One day, in the midst of his
meditations, the Holy Mother appeared to him.

'I have come to grant your prayer,' she told him.

The man explained that his interests had changed, and
that he no longer wanted wealth or comfort.

'But one thing I would like to know,' he ventured.
'Why has it taken you so long to hear my prayer?'

'I knew your prayer before you prayed it,' she replied.
'Out of my love for you I refrained from granting it.'

And the man understood exactly why she had done so.

To learn patience is to put time in its proper
perspective. For many of us today, time has become our
taskmaster. We are driven by deadlines and timetables,
anxious that there is not enough time available to us to carry
out all that is needed. And yet it is only in the last few
hundred years that any accurate measurement of time has
been available. It seems the more we measure it, the less
there is available for us to use. 'Time management' is an

expression of our desire to control time, to make it a functional accessory in our quest to master the world. Paradoxically, the more we seek to exploit time, the more it becomes a prison for us by setting the hard boundaries of our lives.

The alternative is, rather than trying to use time, that we respect and honour it. This can be achieved ritually by the act of what some people regard as 'wasting' time, and what I prefer to regard as 'enjoying' time. That is, to become aware of the sheer pleasure of existence and the force of its movement through us, by unplugging from the external framework of minutes and hours. How long does it take to eat a meal? How long does it take to heal a wound? How long does it take to forgive a wrong? In such questions we confront the absurdity of using time as the sole measurement for human existence. When we are able to relax and release our tight grasp on time, it becomes our gentle companion rather than our relentless enemy. We find ourselves able to allow time to pass, without agonising over what we have 'lost'.

Waiting does not need to be a source of frustration, but can become the way in which we honour existence and its enticing lure. Far from the bleak monotony portrayed by Beckett's *Waiting for Godot*, we may discover in devotional patience a rich landscape of wonder and joy.

Uncoupling from a world that in many instances seems driven, we are able to make a creative gap in which the soul can breathe and God can speak. It is the womb of the imagination; the space from which all that is lasting will arise.

THE BLADE OF THE MOMENT

There is something deeply embedded in the human condition which makes us shy away from the very thing we need most. We fill our lives with noise and distractions as a means of escaping the peace and solitude which we claim to be desperate for. Perhaps we are scared of the honesty which being still faces us with. Or it may be that the attractions of the surface are more appealing than the silence of the depths. Anyone who has tried to pray or meditate will be aware of the inner resistance in the early stages, the perverse reluctance to enter a space in which we are free of other noises. Only by persevering are we able to find our way to the silence our souls so hungrily seek.

In a similar way, our relationship with the ever-flowing stream of time is limited by a desire to escape the blade of the moment. Rather than being fully present to whatever is around us, we have an innate tendency to flee from that sense of encounter. Whether it is to the security of the past or the anxiety of the future, our minds are constantly exploring any other territory than that which lies immediately before us. In so doing we retreat from the fullness of experience, preferring the phantoms of that which is gone or not yet here to the embrace of life in real time. By retreating from the moment, we not only impoverish ourselves, but everyone else we engage with yet never fully meet. Once again we become our own worst enemies by anaesthetising any possibility of spiritual life.

I once spent a week in a Franciscan friary, learning to be quiet. After an initial period of introduction, all of us present on the retreat entered into silence. It took several days before the static of inner voices began to subside. All of my senses were intensified as I cleared my soul of distractions. And then one morning, while sitting at a dining table eating breakfast, I had a remarkable experience. A shaft of sunlight slanted through the window and lighted on a bowl of fruit in the centre of the table. In that one instant, I became fully present, and my heart leapt within me. No description will do justice to the way the fruit glowed, or the soft warmth of the sunbeam, or the pure joy which flooded me in that moment. Suffice it to say that that one second of insight was powerful enough to have stayed with me all these years since.

Nothing, of course, had changed in the physical

universe. On many other mornings the fruit had been present, and the sun had no doubt shone upon it. But I had never seen it before. I had always been somewhere else, in a world of thoughts and distractions of my own making. In that one glorious instant, I suddenly became alive to the world, rather than sunk in a protective numbness. That was my awakening to the overwhelming beauty which is constantly flooding our perceptions, and which is just as regularly ignored. I began to understand how much of my life up to that point had been lost through my own inattention. I had been a dragonfly, skimming across the surface of life and never plumbing its depths. But in just one instance of the eyes of my soul being opened, all of my perceptions of life changed.

It is said of Buddha that he was once asked what it is that makes a person holy. He replied that every hour consists of a certain number of minutes and every minute contains a certain number of seconds. Furthermore, he said, every second contains a certain number of moments. 'Anyone who is totally present in one of those moments knows holiness,' he explained. Jesus counselled his followers to take no thought for the coming day, but to be absorbed by the demands of the present one. Because of our limitations, we have no means of influencing either the past or the future, save by influencing the present. And there is little hope of doing that unless we are willing to come out of hiding and embrace it.

My dog, the generous spiritual director, teaches me what it is to focus on the present moment. When there is mention of either food or a walk, he becomes entirely still. Nothing whatsoever can disturb his attention to the offer at hand, and he is completely absorbed by it. His entire canine being is concentrated and alert, with no thought of what food he may have already eaten or what walks he might get tomorrow. He is a wonderful model of contemplation. To contemplate is not to be involved in some strange ritual; in essence it is to fix attention on that which lies before us, rather than being seduced by other affairs. Thomas Merton described contemplation as 'a sudden gift of awareness, an awakening to the Real within all that is real'. He understood it very simply as 'spontaneous awe at the sacredness of life, of being'.

Such awareness is only possible when we wake from our preoccupied stumbling through life and enter into the crucible of the moment. There is a certain irony in that most of what we seek in life is right in front of us, waiting to be recognised. It calls to us in fact, but we remain deaf to the invitation as long as we retreat from active awareness. In a mysterious way, the whole of our lives is determined by our response to a single moment; and yet we are frequently too absorbed by the pattern of living to participate in it. Joy comes not through evasion of the present, but by wholehearted engagement with it. But in order to achieve this simple attitude, we have to overcome the relentless onslaught of tempting distractions. People who are seeking to achieve focus often sit for long periods observing the single flame of a candle. If they do it for long enough, it enables them to see.

My ongoing journey of discipleship under the tutelage of my dog has given me a little insight into my own predilection for escape from the moment. On our daily walks beside the sea, Baxter has two tendencies which make progress difficult. One is to strain on the leash, desperately eager to rush ahead and get to his destination. Should he see another dog in the distance, he leans forward and tries to pull my dead weight behind him to reach it more quickly. This detracts from the pleasure of the walk, and threatens to increase the length of my right arm. But in such circumstances it is even more difficult than usual to communicate with my dog, such is his state of preoccupation with that which lies in the distance.

The equal and opposite tendency arises when we pass some point of unusual interest for him. Usually this is in the form of a scent which holds deep fascination for Baxter, but which I am oblivious to. In these instances he stops and wants to spend several minutes savouring the identity of whichever of his compatriots has created the canine signature in question. Often he is keen to add his own thimbleful of graffiti to the fence or post at hand. I am singularly unsympathetic to such pastimes, and end up dragging on the lead to encourage him to resume our objective of walking. He becomes a dead weight, conveying his reluctance to be moved on through passive resistance. It takes some urging to get him moving again.

The human equivalent of pulling on the lead is the temptation to flee into the future. We seek to prepare for it by rehearsing various scenarios in our minds, anticipating existence before it has arrived. The commonplace name for the pessimistic version of this is worry — the insistent anxiety in regard to imagined futures. Not only is worry a fruitless loss of energy and calm, it leads us away from participation in the moment, where the real future is actually created. By neglecting the choices that actually lie before us, we invoke the very situations we have imaginatively constructed for ourselves. Our fears become self-fulfilling. Nor is the more positive form of utopian rush towards time's horizon any more satisfying. It is a difficult thing to learn (and seemingly paradoxical) that no future can be better than the present. To strain forward to get to easier times is as self-defeating as Baxter's pulling on the leash.

Others of us prefer the past as a hiding place. Nostalgia has become a universal preoccupation in the face of a world which changes too quickly for our liking. There are those who prefer to dwell on memories and past experiences rather than to create new ones. It is common for people as they age to take up residence in the realm of the past and give up on the challenges of the present. However, this relishing of the bygone is not the preserve of the elderly; it is used as an escape route by many who simply find the raw experience of the moment too demanding. We can easily begin to treasure and incubate old grievances or old joys, to the extent that they begin to determine what our lives become. The past can no more be re-entered or influenced than can the future, and the attempt to do so is ultimately frustrating and potentially crippling.

 The story is told of a young man who desired to become pure. He refrained from eating meat, remained celibate, and lived a blameless life. To deepen his faith, he went into the forest to learn from an old man who was recognised as a wise and holy teacher. One day this respected sage invited the young disciple to accompany him on a trip to a distant village. On their way, they came across a beautiful woman who was in some distress. The river was in flood, and she needed to cross it but was anxious about being swept away. The old man listened, and

without thought hoisted her onto his back and carried her to the other side. When he had done this, the two men continued their journey without speaking.

But the young disciple was fuming. Didn't his master know that contact with women was regarded as defiling? And it was particularly scandalous that he should have embraced a woman as beautiful as that one had surely been. As they walked together, he could not get the image of the old man carrying her out of his mind. After some time, his teacher noticed the sullenness of his devotee and enquired what the problem might be. Glad of the chance to unburden himself, the young student poured out his disappointment over such wilful defilement and breach of etiquette. 'Oh,' replied the master, 'are you still carrying her? I left her on the far bank of the river.'

Neither past nor future provide legitimate respite from the challenge and beauty of the moment. When we learn to become fully present in every instant, we discover that there are opportunities and choices immediately before us which will determine both our past and our future. Here, on the sharp blade of the moment, lie opportunities to create and to love. Equally present are the possibilities of abuse and cruelty. In the capsule of experience which is given to us each instant, we determine who we are and what is significant to us. The whole of our lives is presented to us in the moment, and each moment is an intersection with eternity in which we decide our destiny and are offered the grace of becoming. All else is illusion.

Jesus invited those who listened to consider the birds of the air and the flowers of the field, to become conscious of how they were absorbed in the art of being and not consumed with anxiety for the future. He suggested that, by learning such lessons, they might open themselves to the presence of God, and that the future would take care of itself.

REDISCOVERING LOVE

I enjoy going to outdoor concerts at night-time, when people have those fluorescent light sticks which they wave around in time to the music. In the darkness these snap lights glow brilliantly in a variety of colours. But by the next day the chemical magic which makes them shine has begun to fade, and they seem very ordinary. The physical shape and size of the plastic container remains the same, but the marvellous luminosity has gone. Some words in the English language suffer a similar fate. They start off blazing with meaning, but constant handling and overuse drains them of significance until they become rather dull and tawdry. Few words in common usage have become so evacuated as 'love'.

The advertising industry has much to answer for in its constant devaluing of once-potent words. Together with film-makers, these icon manufacturers have succeeded in diluting the concept of love to the point where it has become insipid and sentimental. Sincere people are now embarrassed to utter the words 'I love you' because the phrase has become as trite and meaningless as 'Have a nice day.' Unfortunately the alternatives are few and often misleading, and so we are faced with the task of recovering the lost heart of a concept which has been emptied and abused. We need to wade through the mire of sop and gush in search of a reality which has the power to turn around the lives of people and the force of empires.

There is a saying from Jesus which is still to be found on war memorials in various parts of the world. It states, quite simply, 'Greater love has no man than that he lay down his life for his friends.' In that stark declaration, and in the context of the suffering and carnage of the battlefield, we begin to draw near to an adequate understanding of what love might mean. In popular culture, as represented by Valentine's Day, love has been romanticised to mean flowers and chocolates. There could be no wider divide than that between this schmaltzy imitation and the bedrock of committed self-sacrifice understood by the Christ.

 A young girl was suffering from a rare form of blood disease. Her only hope was to receive a transfusion from someone with exactly the same blood type as hers. After testing various

members of the girl's family, it was discovered that her ten-year-old brother had a precise match. The doctor talked to him, and gently raised the possibility of his providing a transfusion for his sister. 'Your sister is dying,' he explained, 'but your blood would be able to save her. Are you willing to give your blood?' The boy hesitated for a moment, and the doctor saw that he was anxious at the prospect. But the lad quickly agreed to the process. After the transfusion, the doctor went to visit the brother to see how he was. 'Tell me,' implored the boy, 'how long until I die?' Only then did the doctor realise his young patient's misunderstanding, and know that he had been willing to give his life so that his sister might live.

Love is not in essence a feeling, though it certainly may generate powerful feelings. Rather it is a commitment to the other ahead of ourselves; a willingness to lay down what we might rightfully claim for the sake of another person. This form of devotion unleashes spiritual power unequalled by any other force in the universe. The apostle Paul, who had been a tough-minded religious zealot, was knocked to the ground by such love and left blinded for three days. Later he was to pen one of the finest descriptions of love ever written:

Love is patient; love is kind; love is not envious or boastful or arrogant or rude. It does not insist on its own way; it is not irritable or resentful; it does not rejoice in wrongdoing, but rejoices in the truth. It bears all things, believes all things, hopes all things, endures all things.

Genuine love is magnificent. It weathers storms and bears pain and suffers abuse, and yet remains strong and constant. At the heart of such love lies the quality of forgiveness; the willingness to experience rejection and betrayal, and yet continue to believe the best of the beloved. Nothing can stand in the way of a force such as this. It is the consensus of all the spiritual leaders who have spoken to humanity that the core of the universe consists of pure unadulterated love. By this they mean that the Force or Power which surges through life is relentlessly committed to our well-being, and gratuitously generous in our favour. God is love, and that is as much as we need to know.

Unfortunately there are few people around who experience genuine love at any point in their lives. Our attempts at love tend to be partial, conditional and self-interested. Many apparently loving relationships are simply expressions of codependency in which the participants find a convenient way of having their own needs met. This is a sadly self-perpetuating system, in that the ability to love freely requires some prior experience of being loved. All of us are hungry for love, and our souls require it, just as babies need regular feeding. Because it is so hard to find, we end up accepting substitutes such as sex or dependency. We may even speak of loving or being loved, when in reality we are resigned to something much less than that. But such self-deception does not penetrate very deeply into our souls, and they will find a way to remind us that we are fooling ourselves.

There is only one source of love sufficient to meet our spiritual hunger, and that is God. Here and here alone do we discover what love is, and how utterly unrestrained it is. It is one thing to acknowledge the possibility of divine love; it is quite another to plunge into those raging torrents for yourself and experience the surging power. No one can encounter it and remain unchanged. The love of God is universally active and available, using all means to lure and seduce us. Why then is it that so few of us know it? Because we have hardened ourselves against love, and so against God. We have learned through painful experience that love requires vulnerability, and vulnerability inevitably leads to betrayal and suffering. Those we have given ourselves to have disappointed us and sometimes used us, and so for our own protection we draw back from love.

At the tender age of eighteen, I suffered a dual shock to my capacity to trust. My parents, who had been married for more than twenty-five years, divorced in messy circumstances. My mother, who I was particularly close to, had been involved in an extra-marital affair. And then, in the same year, I was deeply hurt by the girl I had been engaged to. I discovered that not only had she been unfaithful, but also that one of the people she was sleeping with was a good friend of mine. Even now, some thirty years later, it is difficult to express how deeply wounded I was by these psychic assaults. Naturally I withdrew into myself, and began to create defences around the mass of pain I carried in my soul. In so doing, I was limiting my exposure to being hurt like that again in the future.

Later in life, when love visited again, I was cautious, suspicious and a little reluctant. Were it not for the fact that I quite separately discovered the love of God, I doubt my capacity to have entered into a completely healthy relationship ever again. But I was fortunate enough to stumble on that unconditional and trustworthy divine love, and because of it was set free to both give and receive human love. Being immersed in such a powerful stream had the effect of purging the resentment which had begun to collect in my spirit, and which threatened to become bitterness. In that astonishing whirlpool, I discovered that I was known and held and loved, and that nothing I or anyone else could do could separate me from that passionate embrace. It abides as the most liberating and transforming experience of my life.

Of course, I have had to work at renewing that encounter with love at various points along the way. I'm not one of those people who walks around in a state of blessed enlightenment with a slightly dazed and joyous look on my face. On the contrary, I have a tendency to depression and have continued to experience rejection and suffering in various forms throughout my life. But the knowledge of God's love has never left me or failed me, and I constantly return to drink at that spring. And each time I do, I learn again that all my fears about inadequacy or stupidity coming between my soul and God are entirely unfounded. This is something that can never be taught, but only experienced. I wish with all my heart that more people would take the time to stop and learn it for themselves.

To know yourself to be loved is to become entirely free. You are no longer dependent on the approval or acceptance or even the company of others for your peace of heart. Not that this makes us withdrawn and aloof. It simply means that we can open ourselves wholeheartedly and without reservation to the people around us, because we are not dependent upon them for recognition. We have discovered more than enough love for our own needs, and are able to allow the stream of it to flow through our own lives and touch others. If we are misunderstood, if we are rejected, if we are let down, if we are attacked — still nothing can diminish the source of love which floods into us and through us from the heart of God. In this is a discovery which we long to share with any who are ready for it.

The wondrous thing about this kind of love is that it is self-replicating. To experience self-giving prodigal love is to be converted by it, in the very best sense of the word. When our own hearts glow with the certainty of being loved, a strange and slow transformation begins to take place. We start to see with the eyes of love. Everything around us, whether it be people or plants or animals or mountains, becomes beloved. We look at others and see their beauty and marvel at them. It seems entirely natural that we should give ourselves in love and do whatever we can to make their lives better. We know in the depths of our souls that, now we are loved, our lives can never be lost or taken away. And so we find it a source of joy to begin giving up our own lives for the sake of others. In this simple act we discover the meaning of love, in all its joy and pain, and the divine spirit flows through us.

The story is told of how Jesus was taken by the authorities and the religious functionaries and nailed on a cross. As he looked out on them, he saw through the eyes of love and prayed that they might be forgiven, as they didn't understand what they were doing. This is the nature of divine love, that it becomes slightly forgetful and dismissive of all that seeks to deny it, for the sake of finding its way to the broken and twisted souls who have become incapable of knowing it. It is towards love that we are all travelling, and our attempts to resist it or hide from it do little but impoverish our own souls. Once we have found it and bathed there, the journey of life becomes much more than an act of survival. It is suffused in grace, and light illumines the path ahead.

LIFE, LIVES, LIVING

Sometimes I worry that I've had déjà vu in a previous life, but given a little time I feel karma again. What are we to make of the claims of reincarnation; that we've all been here before, and that we may indeed come back for another round of existence? Is that prospect a cause for celebration or despair? Increasingly, it seems, people report recovered memories of earlier lifetimes, sometimes describing historical events from the perspective of an eyewitness. And many religious traditions regard human life as an ongoing cycle of existence. They regard reincarnation as the evolutionary process of the soul, providing renewed opportunities for learning wisdom and humility. Christians, on the other hand, subscribe to the 'one strike and you're out' theory. Personally, I prefer to remain agnostic as to what lies beyond the doors of death, despite several persistent intuitions.

Two monks lived in a remote monastery and became close friends over many years. As the time of their respective deaths approached, they made an agreement with one another. A commitment was made that whichever of them died first would come back to pass on a message to the other as to what lay on the other side. They agreed on a signal: one knock on the wall would signify that everything was as they had been taught and imagined it to be, while two knocks would suggest that things departed from expectations. The day came when one of the monks died. The other could hardly sleep, so excited was he by the prospect of communication from beyond death. Eventually, sometime past midnight, there was an eerie presence in the room. The old man listened hard, and heard a distinct knock. 'Ah,' he said, with a smile on his face. But then followed a second knock. The smile slipped. And then, unexpectedly, a third knock, and a fourth and a fifth... Eventually the monk cried out for the knocking to stop. 'I've got the message,' he confessed.

On the face of it, the issue of whether we have just one shot at life or many makes an enormous difference to the way in which we regard it. If this life should turn out to be all that we have, then it provides a certain focus and urgency to getting things sorted. However, if this is just a staging post on our soul's long journey into eternity, then we may be able to relax a little, confident that there will always be another chance to rectify our shortcomings. But, in reality, the seemingly divergent perspectives turn out to have a similar focus. Both contend that the path to wisdom involves treating this life which we are living as the opportunity for salvation. Even the most ardent advocates of reincarnation see its relentless cycle as something to be broken out of, rather than as a retreat from responsibility.

It may be that we have lived other lives in the past. For me, the jury is still out. Trans-generational memories may turn out to be the product of the collective unconscious. And there is the sheer mathematical problem of where souls come from, given the burgeoning world population; at least some of us must be new models. Whether or not we have had other existences prior to this one becomes somewhat irrelevant when we accept that it is our present life that challenges us to spiritual growth and enlightenment. Pascal used to speak of life as a gamble; those who hold it to be enchanted are betting on the existence of something beyond death. If they should be wrong, they have lost nothing. But if they should prove to be right, then they will be perpetually grateful for not having bet on the opposite prospect.

To acknowledge the importance of our present life is to see it as a sacred gift which would be desecrated through squandering. It is to treat the gift with respect, to refrain from abusing or debasing it. Boredom is a violation of that which is intended to be treasured, as is the constant desire to escape from the complexities of existence. We have all seen the young child who receives a special gift that is quickly discarded in preference for playing with the empty box it came in. The same attitude seems to persist into adulthood for a good number of people, who set aside the chance to become fully alive for the sake of entertainment and distraction. The embrace of life requires attention, involvement and gratitude. Without these qualities we dishonour ourselves and fritter away our days.

It has been said that in drawing one full breath we may discover all there is to be known. In living one full life, then, we have the opportunity to become very wise indeed. The biggest barrier we face to participation in life appears to be the contemporary trend to avoid pain. No child draws breath without a mother's pain, and this is an indication of what follows. There is simply no possibility of vital life without the corresponding embrace of suffering. The besetting sin of our lives is the temptation to anaesthesia and the temporary comfort of numbness. It represents a withdrawal from the challenge of making our way forward. Pain cannot be avoided in life. Even the most enlightened soul cannot escape from it, for love inevitably gathers it in.

Those who love greatly suffer greatly, and those who accept suffering find an equivalent capacity for joy. The way forward in life can never lie in retreating from it, however attractive the prospect may be at times. To parody a former American president, the secret of life involves inhaling, rather than refraining from it. Time and again, we need to summon the courage to walk forward, to 'seize life' and the stimulus to growth which it provides. To do this is to accept and bear the consequences, which may not be what we expect or desire. But it is also to dignify the gift of our own existence. It is to participate, to be active in the forging of destiny rather than passive observers. When my dog sees water, whether a river or the sea, he can't restrain himself from plunging in, and damn the consequences. It's hard not to enjoy his enthusiasm, and to learn a little from it, even when he comes and shakes himself dry at my feet.

The crucible of life is choice. In each day of our living, we discover the intersection of two powerful forces: that which is, and that which is not yet. And we find ourselves standing plumb in the middle of that crossroads. Through the power of decision-making, we forge that which is not yet into that which is. Here we encounter a fundamental mystery — that even though our lives come to us as gift, we fashion them for ourselves. We make ourselves into the people we are, and along the way we give shape to the world around us. Naturally there are circumstances we have no control over, but even then, the way that we respond to such circumstances determines who we will turn out to be. In making such choices, we are continually and progressively choosing between life and death.

In all of our choosing, there is a range of options open to us. The legacy of the past pushes us in a certain direction, which is to recreate more of the same. The easy path is to continually move in a straight line, opting for what is familiar and safe. But among the range of possibilities which confronts us, there will be one that represents the divine lure to go against convention and to make something radically new of ourselves and our world. Often it will hover quietly in the background, and its very novelty will make it appear crazy and ill-advised. But, in the moment of decision, we are given the chance to choose for or against creating life. This freedom contains huge responsibility for working with or in opposition to the gentle Spirit which breathes through existence.

 There is a profound biblical story in which a wealthy man comes to Jesus, wanting to follow him. He is attracted, perhaps, by the freedom and honesty portrayed by the enigmatic man from Nazareth. After some interchange, Jesus recognises his questioner as a devout and spiritual seeker. He suggests to the

man that there is only one thing lacking, and advises him to sell
everything he has and give it to the poor, and then to join in on
the journey which Jesus is pursuing. We are told that the man
went away in great sorrow, because his wealth prevented him
from making that choice. We hear no more about the man,
because there is nothing more to hear. In that crucible of
choosing, he has rejected the path of life as being too costly
and impractical. And then the moment has gone, and he is
consigned to resuming his life of comfort.

Procrastination and timidity can easily become
the enemies of life, representing covert strategies for the
avoidance of choice. Reluctance to commit seems to be
endemic today, and not only in the sphere of relationships.
The reason is not hard to find. In every choosing there is a
small death — the death of possibilities. We prefer to keep
our futures vague and our options open, in the hope that
this may preserve our personal freedom. Abstinence from
commitment and decision seems a mechanism for keeping
the future at bay. Ironically, the reticence to choose brings
about that which is feared most — the tyranny of recurrent
experience. The only hope of breaking unproductive cycles is
to choose outside of them, and commit ourselves to a new
and potentially difficult path. Here is a fundamental mystery
which is built into the fabric of the universe: life comes

through death. In the context of decision-making, our pilgrimage forward into that which we might become requires the death of other options.

For many years I longed to be a writer. I loved words and using them, but circumstances seemed to conspire against me. I had a marriage and children; I had paid work to perform; I had no time available to me. And yet still I dreamed of writing. The dream became something of a comfort blanket to me, and I would suck on its corners and feel sorry for myself that I was consigned to a life where I was unable to do that which I most wanted to. And then one day it came to me that if I wanted to be a writer, I had to choose to do so. It required me, at a bare minimum, to begin writing (recipe for rabbit stew: first, catch a rabbit). Eventually it involved being willing to forgo a regular income, and to spend large amounts of time in a small room with only my imagination for company. Today I marvel at filling in a form and identifying my occupation as that of 'writer'. It is only true because I have chosen to fulfil a dream, rather than to go along with the status quo.

Whether we have one life or many, this is the life which demands all our love and attention. When we come to its end, how will we look back on the way we have responded to it? Each day presents us with new lessons to be learned, new people to be loved, new choices to be made, new opportunities for growth. Those who are told they have a limited period of time left to live discover that each day is imbued with glory and preciousness. They learn to value and savour each passing moment, and not to let the sun go down on discontent or rupture of love. And yet all of us are on our way towards death, whether we are aware of it or not. By learning how to live conscious of that horizon, we may find it marks an invitation to a life richer than our imaginations can contain.

JUST TRAVELLING

When the inner life becomes detached from the outer life, it easily descends into narcissism. The word 'integrity' indicates wholeness, and to achieve it requires balance and harmony between private and public life. That which we claim to be aware of in our souls must become visible before it is credible. Likewise, our actions in the world need to spring from the depths of our spirit if they are to be of substance and significance. Many current forms of spirituality appear to focus on the inner life as if that were sufficient in itself. Without care, this can promote a smug self-love which has no outworking in behaviour. Love is not love at all until it is tested by the Other, and no love is worthy of the name which does not respect and strive for justice.

Nothing seems further from the spiritual life than the realm of politics, and yet, until there is some fruitful dialogue between the two, the fate of the human race will not be hopeful. Politics is a dirty and messy business, and those who enter it are quickly besmirched. On an entirely practical level, however, the application of love and justice to communities entails encounter with the political sphere. People such as Ghandi and Martin Luther King have demonstrated that it is possible to pursue justice in the public realm as the outworking of a predominantly spiritual motivation. As we proceed along whatever path is set before us, we should be careful not to ignore the plight of those who languish at the roadside. If our desire for progress causes us to pass them by, we can be sure that we have neglected our own welfare as well as theirs.

'No man is an island,' declared John Donne. He might be surprised to find that much of current Western society is based on a belief directly the opposite of his claim. The hyper-capitalism which pervades our life imagines that the best way for an economy to grow is for each individual to pursue their own selfish ends. This seems to work well for those who have the skills and resources to participate. But a quick tour through the central areas of our major cities reveals that such success comes at a high cost to those who cannot keep up the pace or are not regarded as having anything to contribute. Walking through the streets of New York a few years ago left me near tears, as the disjunction between the beggars and opulent wealth shouted but was not heard. To make ourselves deaf to the cries of our sisters and brothers in need is to do violence to our souls.

A couple with a small son lived in a cottage. They made a reasonable living for themselves, but had little left over for extras. It so happened that the wife's father was widowed and left alone. Somewhat reluctantly, the couple invited him to come and live with them. He gladly accepted. The couple became intolerant of his ways, especially at the dinner table, where he would tell old stories and jokes, and slip extra food to his grandson beside him. Over time the old man grew a little feeble in mind. He forgot what he had said a few moments ago; sometimes he even forgot where he was.

What upset his daughter and son-in-law most was that he became a noisy and messy eater. He would slurp and belch and spray food out of his mouth onto the table. Oftentimes he would raise his plate to his mouth to scoop food into it, and because his grip was weak he frequently dropped the plates and broke them. Eventually, in frustration, the couple banished him from the dinner table to sit at a small table in the corner of the room. They gave him a wooden bowl to eat out of so that it wouldn't shatter when he dropped it. Their young son was sad to have lost his grandfather from the table.

One day the boy's mother came across him carving a piece of wood with a knife. 'What's that you're making?' she asked her son. 'Oh,' said the boy, 'I'm carving some bowls out of wood so that I will have them ready for when you and father reach old age.' Slow tears fell down the cheeks of his mother. From that night on, they invited her father back to the table, and gave him fine china to eat from.

The key to justice lies in the recognition that whatever happens to the poorest or least of those around us happens to us all. No external force can make us feel responsibility for the lost and vulnerable in our world; only the inner constraint of love is sufficient. We are bound to our sisters and brothers by our common humanity, and attempts to evade this bond wither our spirits. The brave new world of economic rationalism represents new depths in the history of the soul. It is a structural denial of our essential mutual existence.

A holy man asked his followers which was the best way to tell when the darkness of night had ended and day had truly come. 'When you can see into the distance and tell a scarecrow from a man,' suggested one. But the guru shook his head. 'Surely day has come when you can see the clock on the tower and read the time,' said another. The holy man told him he was wrong. 'Well then, how can you tell day from night?' they asked him. 'When you look into the eyes of any man or woman, and recognise

there your brother or sister, then day has come. If you cannot do this, however brightly the sun might be shining, it is still night.'

Love and generosity overcome selfishness, and open a space in our hearts where the homeless may find refuge. Simple acts of compassion count for much more than words or advice. But the key to defeating greed is seeing beyond the false division between them and us. In the end, there is no 'them', only 'us'. Some years ago I became involved in a group which provided housing to ex-psychiatric patients. For me it was an act of charity and practical mercy. Over time, however, the people we were supposed to be helping became my friends and shared their lives with me. They taught me what true humility and generosity were, and I came to understand that I was the one in need of help and understanding.

Justice is a particular form of love, in which we recognise that certain ways of living are at the expense of others, and seek ways of changing that situation. There are inevitably issues of power involved in correcting such imbalances at the public level, and so conflict will often ensue. It is a rare skill to be able to endure the tensions of working for justice without adopting aggressive tactics or harbouring hatred. But, as water shapes rock, there are ways of gentle resistance which are still capable of achieving change and liberation. Preserving love for your perceived enemies is both an essential safeguard and a daunting challenge. A wise person will understand that the lasting means to overcoming strength is to meet it with a persistent and resolute vulnerability, and be willing to absorb whatever violence is necessary to initiate change.

In 1991 I participated in a movement to stop the City Council of Auckland selling off its central city rental stock. My involvement came directly from my friendship with psychiatric patients and other low-income tenants. The council had built the units with low-interest money from government, and in order to replace a slum which it had previously cleared. From its earliest days, the new accommodation had been tagged for people who found the inner urban area too expensive to live in. But the council was short of money, property prices were escalating, and the temptation to sell off the units was too great — even if it did mean the displacement of a community of people who had nowhere else to go. We protesters did all the conventional things: printed posters, organised petitions, wrote letters and submissions, attended council meetings and made representations.

The day came when I attended the final council meeting at which the decision was to be made. Listening to the discussion, it became obvious that the councillors had already made up their minds, and were prepared to sell the properties. In my despair, I was overcome by divine madness. Without forethought, and to the surprise of the gathered dignitaries, I leapt into the centre of the circled benches and began to disrobe. As I removed my clothes, words came to me. I said to the councillors that this was what they were doing to the poor: removing what little dignity they had left and leaving them naked and vulnerable. You think that nobody is watching, I told them, but God is watching, and you are accountable for your decision.

I was left standing in my boxer shorts, wondering what to do next, when the mayor thankfully called for a cup of tea. Later the councillors voted to sell the housing anyway, but the resultant publicity made them shy away from enacting that decision for another seven years. Afterwards, I felt a little ridiculous when I had to go home and explain to my wife what I had done. But, in some ways, my confrontation of the ruling powers with my own vulnerability was a more effective means of achieving change than all of our more conventional democratic attempts. For me it had become a spiritual issue, and required some more imaginative strategy than sheer confrontation. The spur-of-the-moment inspiration struck me as either perceptive or psychotic, and I was not sure until the dust settled which it had been.

We cannot ignore situations of injustice which sit on our doorstep without debasing our own humanity in some way. For all our cleverness at making justifications for ourselves, our souls know that failure to act makes us complicit. We do not all need to be leaders of marvellous campaigns which address high-profile issues. Most of us have plentiful situations which we encounter in the course of our everyday lives where we face the choice of speaking up in the name of justice or remaining silent. Sometimes we draw back from involvement for fear of the consequences that might follow. This is the point at which our spiritual lives can assist us; when we know we are loved, and that nothing anyone can do can damage or lessen that love, it is so much easier to risk our own safety for the sake of others.

It is a very old tradition, rehearsed in stories from diverse religious traditions, that God comes to us in the form of the stranger. On this understanding, it is a dangerous thing to dismiss people we come across in life as being unworthy of our attention. Extending hospitality or generosity may be a means of inviting the divine presence into our own lives, and may result in great blessing for us. Making room in our lives for strangers requires that we create some space for them to come into. The creation of an inner sanctum is thus both a spiritual discipline and a practical act of love. Justice is the extension of this sense of hospitality to the whole community, so that society can graciously include those who have no one else to look out for them. Perhaps then we might learn what it means to have entertained God without knowing it.

LETTING GO

On the beautiful island of Crete
was an old man who had
lived all his days there.
He was deeply
contented
in his life,
and constantly
grateful for the
place in which he lived.
Everything about Crete
seemed to him to be wondrous.
He loved the way the sun sparkled
on the Mediterranean and made it glisten
like diamonds. He loved the sound of the wind
rustling in the trees behind his house. He loved the special
quality of the light around dusk, when all the colours seemed to
glow in gladness. He loved the birds which would come down to
visit him, and sometimes feed from his hand. He loved the smell
of the rich earth after a rainfall. Every day he would remember
to give thanks for the beauty of the island.

Eventually the time of the man's death approached,
and he began to make preparations. When the end was very
near, he had his children carry him outside and lay him down
on the ground which was so precious to him. As he drew his
last breath, he reached out and grabbed a handful of soil from

his beloved Crete, and he died a happy man.

He immediately appeared outside the gates of heaven, clutching his soil. God came out to meet him, in the form of an old man with a long white beard. After all, he didn't want to frighten the newcomer. 'Welcome,' said God. 'You have lived a long and fruitful life, and now the time has come for you to enter into the joys of heaven which have been prepared for you since before you were born.' And God took the man by the arm, and led him towards the gates of heaven. As they approached the entrance, God turned and said to the man, 'There's just one thing. You can't bring that soil into heaven — you'll have to leave it out here.' A look of desperate horror passed over the man's face, and he leapt back. 'Never!' he said. 'I'll never let go of Crete.'

Sadly, God entered heaven alone. Some eons passed, as they do. Once again God came out to see the man, this time in the form of an old drinking buddy. He sat down with the old man, and they quaffed a few beers and swapped some stories. Then God said to his friend, 'Come on, mate. We've been waiting for you for ever in heaven.' And he took the man by the arm and led him once more towards the gate. But, as they approached, God again warned the man about the soil, and again the man refused to enter heaven without his handful of Cretan soil.

More eons passed. God came out once more, but now in the form of a favourite granddaughter of the man. He was overjoyed, and hugged and kissed her. For some time they played games together. And then she said, 'Puleeeze, Grandaddy, we all miss you so much and we've all been waiting for you in heaven. Please come with me.' And she took her grandfather by the arm and led him towards the gates. Well, by this time the old man was growing very old — he'd been camped outside heaven for a long time. As he made his way towards the gate, his strength gave out. Despite his best efforts, he could no longer hold onto the soil he had been treasuring. His fingers fell open, and the earth trickled out between them, into oblivion.

The old man was distraught. He entered heaven as a broken man. But, as he entered heaven, what do you think was the first thing he saw? His beloved island of Crete, of course, prepared for him since before the beginning of time.

That story is perhaps my favourite one in all the world. It speaks to me of many things: the beauty in the world, the hope of heaven, and the tenderness and patience of God. But most of all it speaks to me of my own attempts to hold that which cannot be held, and my reluctance to let go. Releasing our grip on those things which we hold to be precious is both painfully difficult and absolutely essential to making progress on the journey of the soul. The whole of life is a process of letting go of possessions, experiences, stages and certainties, for the sake of making our way forward into the unknown. Learning how to do it without destroying ourselves prepares us for the final act of release: that of letting go of life itself and surrendering ourselves to death.

Relinquishment does not come easily. At the age of five I was furious when my favourite trolley was confiscated by a zealous teacher at school. When I was ten, my dog and best companion in the whole world was shot for worrying sheep. I cried for the best part of a day. By the time I was eighteen, my parents' long marriage fell apart, and it shook me to the core of my being. Shortly afterwards, when my fiancée went off with another man, I turned the pain in on myself and began to use drugs. And all of this was only the beginning of a life in which there would continually be the need to loose my hold on that which I loved and move forward. My life is no different from yours; all of us who make our way in the world face the constantly renewed prospect of loss.

One of the worst possible reactions (though understandable) is to seek to hold onto that which is slipping away from us. It is as futile as gathering snow on a mountaintop to take home in order to have a souvenir of the experience. We have all met people (and may even have been them) who are stuck at some point in their journey because of a refusal to let go and move on. That which we cling to becomes corrupted because of our attachment to it, not to mention the damage done to our own souls. It is necessary to learn to allow the river of life to flow through us, and not to cause it to become stagnant. The desire to clutch handholds in order to resist the current is ultimately self-defeating. As Jesus is reputed to have said, 'Those who try to hold onto their life will lose it.'

There was a father who had two sons. He wanted to teach them to make their way in the world, and so he summoned them and told them that he was going on a voyage, and would be away for some time. To each son he presented ten pounds and a loaf of bread. They protested that this would not be enough to sustain them during his absence, but he would hear none of it. 'I will return in three months,' he told them, 'and I will expect to be repaid what I have given you.' They considered him harsh, and did not understand the love he had for them. They had no choice, however, but to accept his deal.

The months passed, and eventually the father returned. He called his two sons to him and asked how they had done. The first described how he had invited his neighbours over to share the bread, and spent five pounds on wine to accompany it. The day after, with only five pounds to his name, he had come across a beggar in the street and given it away. The second son, who considered himself more responsible, jumped in to report to his father that he had taken steps to preserve what had been given to him, and was in a position to be able to return it.

'Very good,' said the father, 'but first I would like to hear what happened to my son who scattered his money abroad.' And so the son explained that one of the neighbours had come over shortly afterwards, and offered him a job at his bakery, which he gratefully accepted. One day, while he was working, the beggar came into the shop and recognised the boy. It turned out that the old man was actually very wealthy but eccentric, and he gave the son a diamond he had been carrying around for years, as a token of gratitude for the boy's generosity. 'And so, father, I have here a thousand pounds which is yours,' he explained.

The father turned to his second son to hear his story. 'Well, I used the ten pounds to buy a special sealable container in which to keep the loaf of bread, because I knew you wanted it back when you returned. I've guarded the bread all through your absence, even though I've had to borrow food from my brother, and I have it here for you.' With that, he began lifting floorboards to reveal a hiding place where the container was concealed. With a great flourish he removed the lid. Inside was a shrunken, mouldy and stinking lump which may once have been a loaf. 'I'm sorry,' he tendered to his father, 'but at least I tried to look after that which you gave me, rather than wasting it like my brother.'

Nothing in life can be preserved unless it is first let go of. One of the challenges on our pilgrimage is to learn how to live with open hands, rather than with clenched fists. Buddhism teaches us the wisdom of detachment. This is the ability to separate our own contentment from events over which we have no control. To be detached is to be disconnected from happenstance. At first consideration, the idea seems a little selfish, and appears to fly in the face of what was said a few chapters ago about seizing life. But it is possible to be fully immersed in the passion of existence, without having the welfare of our souls determined by circumstance. The secret of detachment is to allow our spirits to be nourished by our inner life, rather than being dictated to by that which happens to us. In reality, far from being selfish, this is only possible through self-emptying.

What we are seeking is to learn how to refrain from grasping, and how to maintain an inner serenity in the face of either good or evil. This is not generated by indifference, but by a recognition that the heart of the universe is good, and that God is love. Therefore we have nothing to fear, and nothing to lose. Surely we will experience pain from time to time, but the force of it should be allowed to flow through us and away; we have to learn to open ourselves to the pain. The common mistakes are either to try to avoid it, or to hold onto it and build our lives around it. The truth is that we often cannot penetrate the meaning of what is happening around us, and detachment allows us to be content with that.

There was a man who lived in a village in China. Although only a poor peasant farmer, he was considered very well off, because he owned a horse which he could use for ploughing and for transport. One day his horse ran away. All his neighbours commiserated with him and exclaimed how terrible this was, but the farmer simply replied, 'Perhaps.'

A few days later the horse returned and brought two wild horses with it. The neighbours all rejoiced at this great good fortune, but the farmer just said, 'Perhaps.'

The next day the farmer's son tried to ride one of the wild horses; the horse threw him and he broke his leg as he hit the ground. The neighbours all offered their sympathy for his misfortune, but the farmer again said, 'Perhaps.'

A few days later government soldiers came to the village to take young men for the army. They rejected the farmer's son because of his broken leg. When the neighbours told him how lucky he was, the farmer replied, 'Perhaps.'

It is wisdom indeed to let go of that which cannot be held, and to hold onto that which cannot be lost, and to know the difference between the two. When we have learned

to relinquish small things, we begin the more serious task of
learning to loose our hold on life itself.

GRACE AND MERCY...

Many elements of life are commonplace: deceit, manipulation, retribution, betrayal, jealousy and revenge. But there is one quality which is always surprising whenever and however we encounter it — that of grace. It is a force so rare that it is difficult to describe to anyone who has not experienced it for themselves. We might speak of grace as the almost physical flow of divine love into and through our lives. Catholics speak of it as if it were some substance like water which could be poured out upon people, and perhaps they are not far from the truth. I believe it is every bit as real and pervasive as gravity, except that the force field of grace draws upward rather than downward. One of the best-known songs across generations is 'Amazing Grace', and the title is well-expressed. Grace is always and everywhere 'amazing'.

One time, when I was hitch-hiking through a remote area, I was dropped off late in the evening and had to hole up overnight in an old schoolhouse. The next morning I rose early and got out on the road. There were few cars, and eventually I sat down and rested outside a farm gate. I played my guitar, and jumped to my feet every half-hour or so as another vehicle approached. I'd been there for some time when a tractor rumbled down the drive. On it was a fairly wide Maori farmer. He approached and stopped the tractor next to me. 'Me and the missus, we seen you sitting out here and thought you might want some breakfast,' he said. And he passed over a brown paper bag which contained sandwiches, boiled eggs, cake and fruit. While I stood there, a little stunned, he carried on: 'My mate should be here in another twenty minutes with the sheep truck. I'll get him to give you a lift through to the next town.'

That was grace in action — totally unexpected and unearned generosity, born out of love towards strangers. I don't even know the name of the farmer. But I do know that what he offered to me on that morning can never be lost. It filled my heart with warmth and joy, and I went on my way with a new perspective on life. That's the power of grace: a sinuous and gentle ability to transform the ordinary into the special. And it multiplies itself. Those who have been recipients of it find their souls suffused with gratitude, and begin to offer it to others. Grace is entirely gratuitous. There is nothing that can be done to earn it or own it. It comes always as a gift, and can only ever be given away. Grace streams into life as eagerly and freely as sunlight, and we find ourselves strangely warmed whenever it touches us.

We all understand how things can go wrong in life. We know why someone who has had a difficult childhood might grow up stunted by it, and end up locked into a negative cycle which produces grief for them and those around them. But, as psychoanalyst M. Scott Peck notes, we have less understanding of why things sometimes move in the opposite direction. How is it that concentration-camp survivors can become not only whole people, but generous and loving? By what process does someone who has been sexually abused as a child grow to be stable, creative and joyous? What power is it that can defy all expectations of disaster, and bring life where we might have only envisaged tragedy?

It is the power of grace, and those who have been brushed by its gentle caress are only too aware that they could not have made it through life without it. Grace represents the quiet entry of the divine into a hopeless situation to transform it totally. In the Middle Ages, the alchemists devoted their lives to finding some magic which would transform base metal into gold. That is the miracle which grace brings, with the one qualification that searching for it is fruitless. The truth is that grace seeks us, and our energy is better spent in opening ourselves to it than in trying to discover and manipulate it.

The question arises why grace seems to suffuse the lives of some more than others. Does this represent a form of divine favouritism? While there is a mystery here that we may never penetrate, there is a sense in which it is possible to close ourselves off to the infusion of grace. If we are supremely confident of managing our own affairs, and plan our lives rigorously, then we are occupying all the territory available. It is an effective way of shutting out the possibility that a benign force may influence our progress and direction. For this reason, grace is more often to be found in the lives of those who confess themselves to be broken and weak. In giving up their own desire for control (even when it has been forced upon them), they create space for healing grace to work the magic of forging their suffering into joy.

 A woman heard a rumour of a secret river in the mountains, where there were diamonds to be found in the water, plentiful as stones. She sold all that she had and bought provisions, and set off into the mountains in search of that river. For many years she explored the rugged terrain, always living in hope of finding the right stream. She listened to the stories of other prospectors, many of whom were aware of the rumoured treasure. But all of the clues she followed led inevitably to disappointment.

The quest kept her going. Always there was the promise
that the very next river she came upon may be the one, and so
year after year she searched. Eventually she began to grow old.
One day she sat down beside a stream and wept. She had no
husband, no children, no friends. And now it was too late in life
to change any of that. She had given up everything, and for
what? A fruitless hunt for mythical diamonds. The woman
cried herself to sleep, empty and broken. When she awoke, the
sun was shining. Its rays glistened across the surface of the
river, and sparkled like diamonds in her eyes. In that moment
understanding filled her soul, and she gave up her search.
Instead, she returned to her village full of joy, and spoke
of a secret place where treasure could be found.

The beauty of grace is that there is neither cost
nor limit to it. It floods our souls relentlessly, once we have
become aware of its presence. To give it away, to share it
with others — that only increases the grace we experience.
Grace in the context of relationships teaches us of another
precious spiritual currency — mercy. Mercy is the voluntary
relinquishment of demands, expectations, rights and
grievances for the sake of love. To receive it when we have
wronged someone is heaven itself; to offer it when we feel
ourselves to have been wronged can be agonisingly difficult.
And yet the two aspects belong together. We cannot give

mercy without having experienced it, and we cannot hope to receive mercy if we are not ourselves willing to offer it to others. As Shakespeare described it so well:

The quality of mercy is not strain'd,
It droppeth as the gentle rain from heaven
Upon the place beneath. It is twice blest:
It blesseth him that gives and him that takes.
'Tis mightiest in the mightiest: it becomes
The throned monarch better than his crown;
His sceptre shows the force of temporal power,
The attribute to awe and majesty,
Wherein doth sit the dread and fear of kings;
But mercy is above this sceptred sway,
It is enthroned in the hearts of kings,
It is an attribute to God himself;
And earthly power doth then show likest God's,
When mercy seasons justice.[6]

Shakespeare is aware that human mercy has its source in God's. We know mercy only because we have been shown it, and once its golden light has bathed us we are set free to be able to live our lives in mercy towards others. This is a spiritual insight that is well expressed in Jesus' prayer, 'Forgive us our sins as we forgive those that sin against us.'

But it is important not to get the cart before the horse. It is barren and frustrating to seek to forgive others in the attempt to win the forgiveness of God. The exact opposite is true, and provides a way forward. God has already forgiven us, and to learn this is the greatest gift of freedom it is ever possible to receive. To understand that we are deeply known, with all our faults and contradictions, and yet loved and accepted, is to be liberated from any accusation which can ever be brought against us. From that fundamental mercy comes our own ability to forgive.

 There was a man who had a particular problem with gambling, which consumed his time and money. When he found himself in debt, he approached his wealthy and generous uncle for a loan, which was granted. But then he invested all the money on a horse, in the hope of finding a quick way of repaying all his debts. Of course the horse lost, and he found himself in an impossible situation. So he went to his uncle and explained what he had done, and threw himself on his mercy. The uncle was saddened, but forgave his nephew the debt.

On his way out of his uncle's estate, the man came across an old friend of his who worked as a gardener there, and recalled that the gardener owed him some money from a small loan made some months ago. The gambler's eyes lit up: here was the chance to get a stake and begin to make some

money again. He approached the gardener and demanded his money back. Unfortunately the man had no money on him, which angered his friend. A scuffle ensued, and the gambler punched his friend and threatened him.

When his uncle heard of it, he called his nephew to him and demanded full repayment of the original debt. 'I forgave you a great deal,' he explained. 'But it seems you cannot forgive the little my gardener owed you. That which you extend to him will also be extended to you.'

Offering mercy is no cheap or easy option. I have suffered the pain of having a family member raped in appalling circumstances. Although the perpetrator was never found, I entertained thoughts of what I would do to him if he was. In my heart I was prepared to murder, to wreak vengeance for the ongoing damage and misery he had caused. The hardest thing I have ever had to confront in my life was whether I could forgive this unknown stranger. Naturally, it was not my place to dispense with justice in regard to his actions. Nor could I absolve any of the legitimate anger of the family member concerned. But for my own soul's progress I needed to consider whether I was willing to let go of my strong instincts for revenge, and relinquish them. After a deep and difficult struggle, I was able to, and so found the freedom to continue my spiritual pilgrimage.

I thought it would crush me to do so. The ultimate source of the eventual giving over of my hatred was the intimate knowledge of the darkness in my own heart, and the way in which that had been swallowed up in the love and mercy of God. I have been forgiven so much, and consequently am called upon to offer that redemption to those who offend against me. Grace and mercy — they are the warm oil in which our good universe is bathed, and they have the power to overcome evil.

AND PEACE

Do we not all seek peace —
that beautiful place of
inner harmony and
tranquillity,
where it is
possible for
our souls to be
in silence and at
ease? Why is it, then,
that with something we all
desire so much, so few are able
to find it? It seems that everywhere
I go, I find people who crave it, and yet
have no clue as to how to achieve it. To find
someone who exhibits an inner silence, and who is truly at
peace, is a rare and valued experience. It seems that, in the
West, most of the population find their lives crowded, frantic,
noisy and fragmented. Everyone is busy, rushing from place
to place as if their lives depended on it. And when we get a
moment's space, the temptation is to immediately fill it with
another task or 'entertainment'.

Small wonder that many find the stress of life too much,
and that mental illness seems to be increasing as a result.

There are a number of misconceptions regarding
peace, which do not help. One is the impression that peace

represents the absence of conflict. Not only is this not true, but conflict is often a by-product of the active spiritual life. To pursue truth in a world of falsehood is to come into contention with those who have a stake in preserving lies. The avoidance of conflict can be a real barrier to the life of the soul, serving as it does to tempt us to dishonesty and manipulation in pursuit of harmony. It may well achieve the absence of conflict, but it will never achieve peace. Peace is not something which is produced by subtraction, but rather by addition. It is a positive quality, a deep inner force which is both powerful and winsome. An empty peace rings as hollow as an empty bottle.

A second misconception is that busyness is a barrier to serenity. We sometimes imagine that peace is unattainable because of the complexities of our lifestyles, as if we have been thrust into a fire and asked to remain cool. We complain that it is impossible. But this understanding is based on the idea that peace or the lack of it is the result of the environment we are in. It is not. Peace doesn't come from outside us, but from the inside. There is no doubt that many people are stretched and pressured by the everyday demands of urban life in the new millennium. Two things can be said about that. The first is that we all have some choice as to what lifestyles we choose to adopt, and must bear responsibility for our decisions. And the second is that peace can be found in any circumstances, regardless of the pace of life.

Yet a third misconception involves the idea that there is some instant path to experiencing it. The increasing use of sedatives and tranquillizers may indicate that some of us seek peace through chemical means. We are seduced by the idea of a calmness which is produced by deadening or flattening our sensitivity to life. This is to confuse peace with numbness. True peace does not arise as a consequence of retreating from life or shutting it out; rather it arises in the midst of engagement with life. This peace cannot be bought or dispensed. It is the spiritual equivalent of physical fitness in that it must be worked at and maintained over a long period of time through intentional discipline.

Even so, peace is not primarily anything that is worked up. Like grace and mercy, peace has its genesis in the good gift of God. We have been made to be in harmony with God, and whenever that is realised peace is generated. It is a by-product of soul-union with the divine Spirit, rather than an end in itself. That is why to pursue peace is always ultimately self-defeating. To use a rather inappropriate analogy, some missiles produce a high-pitched wail when they lock onto a target. In a similar way, our souls exude peace when they have engaged with God and been overwhelmed by love. It might be described, more aptly, as the fragrance of satori.

A disciple asked his guru, 'How am I to attain peace when there is so much noise around this village? Every time I try to meditate, there's a rooster crowing or a child crying or a dog barking. I can't concentrate on my prayers.' The guru said nothing, but took the man by the hand and led him into the forest. They walked for some time until they came across a small pool. It was a windy day, and the surface of the pond had become choppy. 'What do you see in the pool?' the guru asked. 'It is troubled,' replied the disciple. His master then bid him dive into the pool, to the bottom. When he emerged from the water, his master asked him again what he saw in the pool. 'It is still and deep,' the man answered. 'So then,' said the master, 'you must learn how to pray from the water.'

To discover peace is to know yourself held and loved in the heart of God. This is the source and secret of it; a deep and untouchable certainty which is harboured in the depths of our souls. It exists there as a great reservoir which can be tapped and drawn upon at any time and in any circumstances. Once we know where it is and how to reach it, peace is always available to us. By slowly breathing our way into it, descending like the disciple into the depths, we can soak ourselves in the vast springs of serenity. In the midst of seeming chaos or confusion, we are always only a few deep breaths away from accessing an inexhaustible peace. When we return to the surface, we carry the tranquillity with us, bringing it as a free gift to those who surround us. It is not our own peace, or anything we can take pride in; it is the peace of God, freely given.

We lose our peace when our attention gets diverted by the choppy surface of life. There is an old story about Jesus which sometimes gets distorted because people ask the wrong questions of it. It concerns a journey with his disciples, travelling from one side of a lake to the other in a boat. The wind came up suddenly, and the waves began to threaten the safety of the craft. Jesus was asleep in the stern of the boat. The disciples were anxious, frightened that the vessel might be swamped at any moment and they would all drown. They woke Jesus and, unperturbed, he turned to the angry seas and spoke to them. 'Peace; be still,' he said, and the waters grew quiet. He then chastised the disciples for their own lack of faith. They had been rattled by the lake's surface, and lost their own basis of peace.

Life presents many opportunities for us to lose our focus, to be caught up in the changing tides and threatening skies of everyday existence. We are constantly warned of threats to our security, whether they be from criminals or rising interest rates or some new virus. Little wonder that we become anxious, and begin to run in ever-decreasing circles in the attempt to stave off disaster. Fear is the enemy of peace, and causes us to lose our concentration. But as we look back over our lives, we realise that the vast majority of our anxieties are entirely without foundation. All of our worrying does nothing to help prepare us for difficulties when they do come — whereas the regular visitation of that reservoir of peace which lies at the core of our being will equip us to face even the most dire events with equanimity.

One of the deep fears which seems to beset people in mid-life is what will become of them in old age. There was a time when the middle years of life were regarded as a time to begin relaxing in preparation for retirement. Now we are lectured like naughty schoolchildren on the perils which will befall us if we don't earnestly engage in stacking away money to sustain us over our latter days. While I don't want to dismiss prudence, it seems to me that we are creating an entire industry based on fear, and one which distracts us from the true tasks of the second half of life. How can anyone know whether they have enough to last them through, let alone what unexpected events may occur in the intervening years?

It is tolerable, I imagine, to reach the end of our days wealthy but spiritually destitute. At least we would have money to distract ourselves from the inner emptiness. But, come that final threshold, when we look across the border of death and realise that we can take nothing with us other than what we have stored in our souls, I wonder how the situation might look? The nurturing of peace, however, is able to sustain us even in the abject poverty we fear most. And, paradoxically, the more we can attain inner quietude and contentment, the more it seems that the material aspects of life begin to take care of themselves. It is not irresponsibility that I am suggesting, but rather giving attention to those matters which are most important in the long view of life.

 A window cleaner paused from his work, and sat on a bench on the side of the street. He scraped out his pipe, and watched the people passing. He enjoyed the vibrant hum of life. A young businessman came and stood near him, waiting for a taxi. The old man asked him if he had any matches. The businessman stopped checking his watch and noticed the cleaner for the first time. He apologised for not having matches, but continued to stare curiously.

'Excuse me,' he said eventually, 'but do you mind if I ask what you're doing?'

'Not at all,' replied the old man. 'I'm having a rest and filling my pipe.'

'But why aren't you busy cleaning windows?' puzzled the businessman.

'Why would I be doing that?' countered the cleaner.

'Well, then you could earn more money. With the money you could buy new ladders and cleaning equipment. That way you would make even more money, and perhaps be able to employ some people to do the cleaning for you.'

'What would I do then?' asked the wily old man.

'Well, then you could really relax and begin to enjoy life.'

'And what do you think I'm doing now?' replied the cleaner, filling his pipe with a satisfied smile.

That which brings contentment to the human heart is not generated outside of it. The movement is quite the contrary: from our inner being into the world. When we have discovered the source of our peace, we become people who can take it to others, helping to calm their anxieties. Sometimes when a child becomes frightened and begins to shake, their parent will pick them up and cuddle them, holding them tightly so that they can feel the stability and safety of their body. In a similar way, the quality of spiritual peace becomes an almost physical force which can be shared with others in the moments of fear and uncertainty. So it is that contemplative people may develop a role as peacemakers — not by setting out to do so, but merely by being present in the midst of trouble, and allowing their souls to soothe those who are disturbed.

Peace on the earth;
peace on tree and flower;
peace on beast and bird;
peace on sea and river;
peace on field and mountain;
peace on every small abode.

Peace on mother and child;
peace on guest and stranger;
peace above, below, beyond;
peace in the heart;
peace for the night;
peace without end.

Amen.

RELATIONSHIPS

For periods of our journey, we travel in partnership with others. Many of us will form deep relationships with fellow travellers along the way, expressing varying degrees of intimacy. When we commit ourselves wholeheartedly to one other person, even for a short length of time, we open ourselves both to new opportunities and new dangers. Here I want to discuss those relationships which go beyond (while hopefully including) friendship, so that there is a sense of exclusivity about the nature of the sharing. While these will often be sexual in nature, they need not be. What is significant is the degree of mutual commitment and respect for the other. The fact that many people 'pair off' in couples is an indication that there is something within our human nature which seeks out the deep love of a single 'other'. And yet, today, there are few who are able to traverse relationships without tragedy and pain.

The term 'soulmates' is evocative of the highest

ideals of relationship. It refers to a companionship in which there is some mysterious coupling of the spiritual pilgrimages of two individuals. I have stood above the junction of two great rivers, and watched how they flowed into each other. It seemed to me to express some of the possibilities of love, as well as highlighting the associated difficulties. The intermingling of deep streams creates a force and power and beauty which is more than that of the tributaries. But when they merge so that they can no longer be distinguished, something important may well have been lost. The interplay between individuality and partnership is the key to relationships that bring life and hope into the world, and are mutually creative. It seems there are few of them around, and that the majority of people experience their attempts at love as uniformly destructive.

If we have not begun the work of knowing ourselves, and understanding the sacred journeys of our own souls, then our relationships will tend to be driven by codependency and an unhealthy craving to have our needs fulfilled. It is well said that the capacity for love depends on a mature self-love — a recognition of our own personal value, irrespective of our shortcomings or failures. To seek out other people in order to plug some hole in our own existence will always be a fragile basis on which to approach intimacy. In its crudest sense, much of the human coupling which takes place at these times is a form of relieving sexual tension, in which the partners offer sensation without any corresponding sharing of their inner lives. When that happens, we belittle both ourselves and our partners, and the magic of love eludes us. We cannot treat people as a means of achieving our own satisfaction without doing spiritual violence.

Love proceeds from self-knowledge. Only when we truly know ourselves are we free to give ourselves to others. And, when that happens, we discover that we are able to give without losing anything. Many of us, however, are tempted into using relationships as a means of avoiding our own inadequacies. Those who cannot bear to be alone, and crave company, are often driven by a reluctance to encounter their own inner emptiness. They use people as a means of distracting themselves from spiritual anguish; some bounce from partnership to partnership as a means of hiding from confrontation with major issues. That can never be a healthy basis on which to build intimacy. Often such needy people seek each other out, and make an unconscious deal to swap neuroses. Occasionally these demeaning relationships last for a long time, but they are hardly a good advertisement for the human ability to love.

When love proceeds from wholeness, it operates in freedom and generosity. Our partners are regarded not as a means to satisfying our own needs, but as the beloved. We give ourselves not out of any inner need, but rather from a desire to bring joy and pleasure to the other. That love may be unreciprocated; and if it is that is of little account. We are not striking a bargain — we are not offering something on the condition of an expected return. It is not that our partner has something we need in order to make us complete. Rather it is that we choose freely and joyously to place the pleasure of another person before our own. Often this generates a response in kind, in that love generates love. But not necessarily, and unrequited love is a familiar theme in literature and personal experience. It is a sharing in divine love, which pours into the world yet is seldom reciprocated.

Young lovers often stare fixedly into each other's eyes, mooning and moaning. We say that they have eyes only for each other, and in that imply a gentle criticism. Relationships which consume people are generally destructive rather than creative. While there is a necessary and sacred inner core to any partnership, when it excludes others by withdrawal there is often something amiss. Genuine love leads to expansion and creativity, and a passionate relationship will often bless and enrich all those who come within its influence. Love drives us outward rather than sucking us into some remote hideaway. A healthy relationship will greatly expand the range of possibilities and friendships available to both partners. In this way it becomes enriching and life-giving, both characteristics of the flourishing soul.

There is a certain tragedy in the way that people are willing to lose themselves in relationship, to sacrifice their unique individuality and to begin to live through the other person, or else through some amorphous joint identity. This is more in the nature of vicarious living than genuine love. It is the submerging of the soul in some other pool, with the risk of drowning. A good test of a partnership is whether it enhances the creativity and personality of both participants. We are never required to lose ourselves in another on a long-term basis, even though there may be exquisite instances of soul-union along the way. Love breathes life into us, and any relationship which is asphyxiating should be suspect to us. As Kahlil Gibran has expressed it in poetry:

Love one another but make not a bond of love:
Let it rather be a moving sea between the shores of your souls.
Fill each other's cups but drink not from one cup.
Give one another of your bread but eat not from the same loaf.
Sing and dance together and be joyous, but let each of you
be alone,
Even as the strings of a lute are alone though they quiver
with the same music.[7]

All relationships have in their early stages an element of power struggle, despite attempts to prove otherwise. When we are on our own we make our own decisions and develop our own preferences. But when our lives become closely linked with that of another person, we find that we need to negotiate in relation to an entirely different set of choices and expectations. Most of us find this initially perplexing. That which we have taken for granted as being self-evident common sense is challenged by interaction with quite different perspectives on what is normal and natural. The usual reaction to this state of affairs involves one or other, and frequently both, of the partners attempting to exert their will over the other. Sometimes this is overt, but more often not. Using many devious means, we find ways of seeking to subtly manipulate the other party into our way of seeing things. And, not surprisingly, before long this results in resistance and conflict.

Conflict is not the end of relationship, but the beginning. It is the first flowering of the realisation that the two people involved are very different from each other, however much they may be in love. Only in the encounter with such difference does the real work begin. Many people despair during this period of psychological trench warfare. Their options seem to be two: either to dominate and exert their own point of view over that of their partner, or else to acquiesce and submit to a choice which they are not particularly happy with. The former achieves victory, but at the cost of equality and freedom. And the latter achieves harmony, but at the cost of trust and self-determination. Sadly, many couples never seem to get beyond these two options, and the respective strategies can harden into permanent roles for the participants, never really satisfying either of them.

Growth occurs with the willingness to give up on such power struggles. Beyond domination or surrender, there lies a third possibility: that of partnership. It comes only when the desire to exert our own will has been relinquished. This is not the same as passivity or compliance. Rather, it arises with the recognition that our partner is not a competitor at all, but a fellow traveller on the journey of life. Instead of feeling threatened by the difference represented by our companion, we begin to marvel at and respect it. We allow them to be who they are in all their mysterious and perplexing otherness, and give up on the attempt to convert them into ourselves. This involves ceasing to attempt to live our lives through our partners, and brings us a new sense of humility. It does not remove our differences, but changes our attitudes towards them. We begin to understand that whatever the way ahead may represent, it will not be achieved by one person winning and another losing.

Perhaps the most difficult quality to achieve in a relationship is that of trust. The experiences of life teach us that people will betray us. All around us are stories of people who are unfaithful, and who treat their so-called loved ones with disdain. We know intuitively that to give ourselves wholeheartedly to another is to risk massive disappointment. And so, as a self-protective mechanism, we tend to hold something back. As well as being involved in the relationship, we simultaneously stand outside of it and evaluate our partner, looking particularly for any signs of deceit. Ironically, this strategy for survival can contribute to the very outcome it fears most. That which is held outside of the relationship as an escape route prevents us from giving and receiving trust. There is no safe way to trust another person. While we can avoid naivety, we cannot vest our lives in partnership with someone else without dangerous exposure to risk. Trust is not a quality formed by standing back and objectively assessing potential liability to pain. It is a gift which is given completely or not at all.

Tragically, it is often violated. Love has no guarantees — it is always and everywhere a venture of faith. As has been said, it is better to have loved and lost than never to have loved at all. Genuine love, far from being safe, will always require that we give to our beloved our entire trust. If it should be betrayed, we will haemorrhage and ache. But, ultimately, it will be the one who has offended against love who must pay the price for it in their own souls. We should look out for our own faithfulness and integrity, and then we will have nothing to fear from loss, even though it be painful. Over time, trust is self-reinforcing. The gift of trust allows its recipient, if they have love in their heart, to act in a trustworthy manner. Something relationships teach us about life is that we can only ever keep that which we are willing to freely give away.

To negotiate the perils of relationship is to encounter the exquisite beauty of another soul, and to share intimacy of a kind that is not easily available in any other way. But, paradoxically, it is only when we are at peace with ourselves that the possibility of such union becomes possible. Whether in relationship or out of it, the inner life is the source of understanding and joy.

SEXUALITY

Some people regard sexuality and spirituality as being at opposite ends of the spectrum. Nothing could be further from the truth. Sex has to do with the deepest core of human existence, where intimacy finds physical expression. Many of the problems we experience with our sexuality today are the result of a debasing of it, so that it is regarded as a casual mechanical activity. Like a number of areas in life, sex becomes what it is imagined to be. If we have a closed view of the universe, where mystery and sacrality are ruled out by definition, then we should not be surprised that sexuality becomes banal. A fixed focus on posture, sensation and genitalia will make sexual encounters a purely animal experience. Not that these aspects are any less important than the notes on a musical score, but if they are our only criteria for evaluation, then we miss something of the deeper essence of the experience.

Sexuality is always spiritual. If we reduce it to

its base elements, and make of this sacred gift a hedonistic device with which to distract ourselves, then we are doing grave damage to our souls. Throughout history, mystics and spiritual pioneers have used the metaphor of sexual union to relate their experiences of the divine. This is neither accidental, nor evidence of some repressed fantasies. Rather, it arises from the fact that the self-transcendence achieved in loving sexual embrace is the closest analogy we have to the encounter of the soul with God. Sex, then, is the highest of human arts; to treat it as a commodity is to devalue both the life of the body and the life of the soul. And yet that is exactly what has happened in Western society. If earlier generations were ridiculed for being prudish and repressed, surely ours can be characterised as being satiated and hollow.

Let us then speak of these deep things that are normally either neglected out of politeness, or misrepresented through prurience. Sex is about intimacy. Most relationships have sexual overtones, even if there is no physical exchange at all. Those who have opted for celibacy in life are not, generally speaking, asexual. Sometimes the absence of bodily expression can enlarge the capacity for intimacy, rather than reduce it. What then is intimacy? It is the touching of one soul by another. Whenever this happens, there is a sexual charge to the encounter. People who train as therapists or spiritual directors learn to be aware of this phenomenon, in order that they can deal with the force wisely and beneficially. Unscrupulous or naive practitioners take advantage of the confusion created, and cross boundaries to the detriment of themselves and the people they are working with. The crossover between sexuality and spirituality is real and common.

When we speak of the 'act of sex', we are talking of what should be the focal point of a thoroughly intimate relationship. Sexuality is a factor which affects all of a relationship; 'making love' gives flesh to and deepens the intimacy which is already present. Often, when relationships get into difficulty, this will be manifest in sexual problems and frustrations. It is a mistake, however, to focus on sexual intercourse itself, as if this could be isolated from the wider fabric of intimacy. Instead, set about repairing the love, trust and respect; then the sex will once again become a delight. It is a symptom of our times that we give so much attention to the physical aspects of sexuality, such as techniques and orgasms, and so little to the spiritual side, which is ultimately both more significant and more likely to increase the joy of the experience.

At the heart of sexual exchange is the act of self-giving. Without that, sex becomes a parody of itself — a selfish and violating intrusion. While there is an obvious physical correlation for women in 'opening themselves' to lovers, in truth the same quality is required of any sexual partner, regardless of gender. In the process, we become extremely vulnerable. We may often be physically naked during our lovemaking, but in sex we are always spiritually naked. Our souls are exposed and defenceless, and so capable of both spectacular rapture or searing pain. The most creative environment for sexual expression is that of love and trust. When it is present, we are able to literally abandon ourselves to our partner, without fear of rejection or abuse. And it is, of course, in total abandonment that we experience absolute ecstasy of body and soul. In contrast, where there is mistrust or misgiving, we hold back something for safety's sake, and the experience is correspondingly truncated.

It is for this reason that the wise advocate committed love as the best setting for sexuality. Not that they are killjoys or moralists, but that they hope to encourage the conditions in which both spirituality and human joy are enhanced rather than diminished. The current sexual climate is one of variety and experimentation, in which many people exchange partners with careless disregard. In so doing they imagine themselves to be 'experienced'. Tragically, all they achieve is repetition of a rather shallow and narcissistic performance, which is devoid of genuine intimacy and therefore of potential for deep satisfaction. Unloving coupling is a parody of real love, on the level of a child banging a tin drum compared with the glory of a symphony. At one level they might both be described as music, but the experiences are wildly different.

At the peak of sexual experience, there is the dissolution of personal boundaries, and genuine melding of two souls. This is, and can only ever be, a temporary experience, but for its duration we enter into a different level of existence. We become aware of our soul's potential for transcendence and capacity for joy. It would be wrong to become fixated on sexual experience as a means of generating this condition, just as it is a mistake to use drugs as the only way of generating meditative states. Instead, it is better to understand sexuality as an analogy for the soul's progress in other areas, and particularly in relation to the divine. That which is possible between humans is also possible between individuals and God. Though it seems almost scandalous to speak of it, the loving embrace of God is overpoweringly passionate and intimate, and those who taste it often revert to sexual categories when trying to describe it. It is only necessary to read some of the writings of St John of the Cross or Julian of Norwich to find faintly shocking allusions.

On the level of purely human sexuality, though, we often seem to fall into difficulties. One of the problems is the lack of frank discussion about our sexual lives. It is strange that, in a culture where sex appears to be the most prevalent part of existence, so little attention is given to our honest conversation about our own experiences. Because of the vulnerability associated with sexual intimacy, it seems that we are reluctant to expose ourselves any further than is necessary. Many of us carry pain and disappointment related to our stumbling ventures into sex, but feel unable to talk even to our partners about such regret. What makes it more difficult is the surrounding climate of expectation, where lovemaking is regarded as a performance, one in which participants must always achieve success. The concentration on orgasm, in particular, puts enormous pressure on lovers. How many articles are there now in magazines on ways of achieving or enhancing orgasm?

Singling out climax as the goal of sex is like regarding dessert as the goal of dinner. It fixes attention on entirely the wrong feature of the experience, and tends to devalue all that comes before it. Far better to focus on the loving pleasure which can be given with the softest brush of one finger on the flesh of another, than to be rushing off to some distant destination with all the anxiety of missing a bus. In order to give ourselves entirely, we need to be relaxed and feel safe. One of the frequently neglected aids to sexual encounter is that of time. Of course it is possible to race from one place to another, and feel quite smug that you have got there so quickly. But those who spend a little time lingering along the way may discover territory and enjoy experiences that would otherwise be missed. All of this, naturally, relates to a total attitude to life and not merely to sexuality. It is the deep inner life which shapes us for the ways in which we will be intimate with others. Soulful lovers will both give and receive greater pleasure.

In sex we learn one of the great truths of the universe — the physical and the spiritual are intimately connected with each other. Any philosophy which suggests otherwise must be suspected of a lack of balance. To be spiritual does not mean to withdraw from life or physical existence. Nor is physical life unimportant to the development of the soul. Eating and drinking can also be fundamental elements of spiritual growth. Through hospitality around the table, we give practical expression to the generosity of our hearts, and provide a safe and loving environment in which strangers may be made welcome. We might go so far as to say that without such expression, hospitality is nothing more than a fine idea. And without an understanding of the importance of hospitality, eating becomes merely a mechanism by which we refuel our bodies.

Physical life and the inner pilgrimage, then, are part of each other and reinforce each other when kept in harmony. The best possible preparation for sex is the continuing refinement of our souls. And lovemaking has much to teach us about spirituality. When equilibrium is achieved between internal and external worlds, we discover that the earth is suffused with soul and that every part of our lives has religious significance for us. This is a useful antidote to the common tendency of people in the West to split life into polar tensions. In reality, our pilgrimages form a seamless unity, in which even the most basic and mundane of functions has some lesson to teach us. Only those who have a special call on their life should retreat from everyday existence for spiritual purposes. The vast majority of us will do better to pursue meaning amid the confusion and clutter of ordinary routines. When wisdom comes, we will realise that there is nothing at all which is ordinary.

Each person is a great mystery. We hardly begin to understand ourselves, let alone others. So, when we meet one another intimately, we are encountering the sacred. In sexual exploration, we are quite literally plumbing the depths of each other; touching the most precious core of another person who is made in the image of God. What a wonderful and marvellous gift this is — how glorious and beautiful the mutual tenderness and generosity of the sexual embrace! If it be true that God is present wherever love is, then it is certain that the divine presence permeates every loving episode of sexual entwinement. Correspondingly, perhaps, to use sex selfishly or unthinkingly is to profane that which is sacred, and therefore to trespass on the borders of blasphemy. People can never be used as a means to an end without some ongoing consequence in the lives of those who transgress against love.

Sexuality is an indicator of both the highest and the lowest potentials of humanity. When the gift is abused, it has the power to corrupt the very core of all that is of value, and to wreak havoc in the lives that suffer under love's sacrilege. Equally, when treated with the dignity and respect it deserves, sex can become a door into deeper participation in the dance of life, and perhaps even a gateway to encounter with God.

AGE AND BEAUTY

Ageing is relentless. It comes upon us whether we invite it or not. One of the deep certainties of life is that each day we will be a little older than we were the day before. Strange, then, that something so natural should have come to be regarded almost as an enemy. People both resist and curse the process of getting older. The very wealthy may succeed in changing appearances for a little while, but even they are eventually forced to confront the realities of age. What is it that we so fear? Loss, certainly. We are anxious about losing our vigour, our taut skin, our status, our acumen, our health and our faculties. And, at a deeper level, it may be that we also fear our approaching death, and try anything to stave it off. Some hold out the hope that technology will eventually halt and even reverse the ageing process. Such hopes are mechanisms for avoidance, and generally neurotic.

The Western attitude to growing older is very

161

negative and in marked contrast to that of some other peoples, where age is imbued with great honour. The emphasis in our society is on the diminishment which ageing brings, with little recognition of the gifts it confers. Among these we might include wisdom, compassion, skill, self-awareness, contentment, security and deep satisfaction. We suffer from an overestimation of the benefits of youth, and a consequent devaluing of age. The truth is that each stage of life has its own unique beauty, and the path to fulfilment lies in appreciation of the particular opportunities which our respective phases of the journey bring. To regret the present and long for the past or future is a barren attitude to life, and results only in misery. In acceptance come contentment and joy; in resistance lie bitterness and disappointment.

 Martin Luther once told the story of a dog which carried a fine bone in his mouth, and felt happy with life. But eventually the dog came to a small still pond, and paused to drink. As he trotted up to the edge of the pool, something caught his eye. Reflected on the surface of the water he saw a dog with a bone. He growled at this intruder, but the other dog simply growled back. The bone which the dog in the water held in his mouth looked altogether bigger and juicer, and the thirsty animal became entranced by it. Suddenly his own bone did not seem so special or attractive. Finally, overcome by envy, the dog opened

his mouth and made a desperate lunge for his rival's bone.
All that happened was that his own fell into the pool with a
resounding splash, and disappeared into the depths. At the
same time the other dog disintegrated into ripples. The hungry
animal went on his way, lost now in regret.

It is as futile for a young person to be impatient
to be old as it is for an old person to wish to be young.
There is never any better age to be than the one you are now.
Once that is accepted, we are free to get on with the job of
understanding what the special demands of our stage of life
are. The tasks of the twenty-year-old are not the tasks of the
fifty-year-old, and it would be fruitless to pursue the same
ends at one age as at the other. It is seldom that the whole of
anyone's life comes into view at the beginning. Mostly we
need to wait until we have reached a certain vantage point
before we can see the section of road which lies immediately
ahead of us. This means that new vistas are continually
opening up on the journey of life. The popular view — that
growing older is a process of gradual closing down — is both
distorted and destructive. In fact, given a life fully lived, the
possibilities for contribution to humanity generally expand
with age rather than diminish.

Youth has its attractiveness, certainly. It is a shame
that many of us don't begin to value it until it has gone.

Sometimes it is only later in life that we are able to appreciate the lithesome energy and freshness contained in youth. The idealism and certainty of this stage of life are wonderful to regard, like the first unfurling of a beautiful rose in the morning before the sun has begun to beat down. Young minds are sharp and young bodies athletic, and the combination allows achievements which may be impossible later on. The vitality of youth spills out across all boundaries in an ungainly celebration of life. It would be repressive and niggardly to burden such freedom and enthusiasm with unnecessary responsibility. The joy of the young is to be young — that is why it is so tragic when experience forces cynicism upon them before their time, and robs them of the lively enjoyment of life. The young are beautiful to behold.

But, if that is true, then it is equally true that the old are also beautiful to behold. When we look deeply into old eyes, and recognise the rich texture of creased skin, we begin to understand the astonishing loveliness of human life. The old carry with them their cargo of experiences, every one a harbinger of wisdom and understanding. The miracle of ageing is that the soul begins to rise to the surface, and becomes visible in the pattern of a person's face. Kindness, patience, tenderness — all these are imprinted in flesh for all to see, as are greed, malice or bitterness. Those qualities which define a person's character become honed and developed as the journey lengthens, and they are not so easily hidden. Where the soul is beautiful, that beauty becomes plainly and compellingly evident. The beauty of the old is complex and layered, like that of a fine wine. Youth seems almost shallow and flashy by comparison. One is not better than the other, however; they are both spectacular in their own right.

There is little doubt that physical attractiveness is closely associated with youth in the eyes of the world around us. This is particularly true for women, and therefore the apparent loss of beauty is regarded by many women as part of the cost of ageing. Perhaps because the male body is less idealised than the female, older men do not always feel the same diminution of attractiveness. My wife constantly tells me that it is easier for me than for her to grow old gracefully, and I understand the influences which seem to suggest that is true. But all of this grows from a preoccupation with outward appearance, and a youth-fixated cultural view of beauty. If it be the case that the soul becomes more evident in later life, and that the soul improves over time when properly nurtured, then in general people might expect to grow more lovely over time. This is undoubtedly so when the eyes of the spirit are used to behold people. The most beautiful person in the world is someone who is at peace with themselves, and that is a condition which often takes many years to achieve.

One of the most critical transitions in the progress of the soul occurs around the middle of life. During this subterranean shift, attention moves from the outward aspects of existence to the inner questions of meaning, significance and spirituality. How we handle this transition can determine the way in which we respond to the second half of life. It is a perfect opportunity to re-evaluate goals and commitments in the light of the certainty of our approaching death. Negotiating the change can prove difficult, as evidenced by failed relationships and assorted crises. It is an interesting time to consider a career change and, if planned responsibly rather than in a reactive rush, has the potential to allow a more intentional and focused approach to life. As maturity comes, we find the freedom to let go of the quest for peripheral matters like status, wealth and comfort, and instead learn to value the qualities of integrity, peace and self-acceptance.

As Carl Jung has pointed out, it is usually only in mid-life that the true self comes into purview. Up until that time, we tend to shape our lives in response to the demands that others put upon us, or else our own internalised view of what image should be projected in order for us to be accepted within our communities. During this phase of our lives, the face we show to the world is something of a construct over which we have only limited control. But, as we reach the mid-point of our lives we find ourselves increasingly dissatisfied with living according to someone else's agenda. Recognising the limited time we have available, we begin to ask what it is that is our unique gift to give or to be. Expressing that which is within us takes on a new and vital significance. For some this will mean making a contribution to social change; for others it may be finding a new creative outlet for some inner artistic urge.

After many years of incubation, the self begins to surface in our consciousness. Sometimes we have donned so many masks and personas that our true self appears to us as a stranger. In a perplexing way, one of our first tasks is therefore to meet with our selves, and learn to own them. Once we have overcome the initial fear this produces, we discover with great joy that we are able to relax into being no one other than the person we have always been. If you are young and reading this, it will make no sense to you at all. But, if you are a little older, you may begin to have a glimmer of insight into the mysteries of the emergent self. There is an astonishing sense of freedom which comes from laying down the expectations of others. We discover that we have nothing to lose, and are not nearly so dependent on the approval or disapproval of the people around us.

We are aware of our faults, certainly — at times painfully so. Part of our new-found maturity enables us to be frank with others about our shortcomings, without feeling that we have to cover them up in the interests of popularity. But at the same time we become conscious of our unique gifts as well, and take a quiet but intense joy in expressing them. We begin to know ourselves thoroughly, and thus we are able to live out of our own centre passionately and without apology. If accolade or reward comes, we are able to accept it with equanimity, neither exhibiting false modesty nor using it as the basis for arrogance. In knowing and accepting ourselves, we become free to love and forgive others. It doesn't seem to require quite the effort it did in earlier times. And if we continue to work at the life of the soul, then we develop an awareness of the overpowering joy and beauty which streams into life on a daily basis, and recognise that our frail life makes its own contribution.

As we age, we grow more at home in our own skin, even if that skin does begin to wrinkle. The peace within us deepens, and we find ourselves able to live out of it in everyday situations. We understand that our certainty about some things is increasing, while about others it wanes in equal proportion. The inner life becomes all-absorbing, and we find ourselves reduced to tears by simple things: a phrase in a poem, a glance from a friend, the song of a bird, the touch of a hand. It may be that we are losing our senses.

But it could also be that we are in the process of gaining them for the first time. We may be developing the beauty of age; a quality which discovers a mirroring beauty reflected from every facet of existence. It is the beginning of a journey into indestructible life.

THE CREATIVE SPARK

The oldest Christian (and Jewish) story is that we have been made by God. My favourite version tells that God scooped up a handful of earth and breathed into it, and out of that act humanity was created. Like all stories, this one carries many possible readings. I have often had cause to reflect on the notion that the best way to understand people is as a mixture of mud and the breath of God. The deepest significance of the tale is that God breathes divine life into the new being. Here we have a fundamental assumption which shapes the way that life is experienced: the understanding that there is something of God within every person. This is sometimes acknowledged by the affirmation that all of us are made in the image of God. When we understand and accept this, then we know that every person is sacred, and that to dehumanise anyone is a transgression against God.

Over the course of many thousands of years, there

has been a lot of debate about the way in which the mark of God is pressed into human flesh. Some have seen it as the ability to use tools, others as the capacity to think. Probably it is not as important to know the precise manner of our reflection of God as it is to know that in some way we carry divinity within us. But, if we are to allow the indulgence of speculation, I would venture to suggest that the quality of humanity which echoes the life of God is that of creativity. Like God, we are capable of bringing into being that which does not yet exist, and of taking great pleasure in that act. In so doing, we become co-creators with God, sharing in the task of making the universe a more beautiful and loving place.

To observe the complexities and subtleties of the natural order is to be aware of the abundantly creative nature of God. In the myriad shades of green of a forest, in the spectacular birdsong which greets the dawn, in the teeming masses of darting fish, in the haunting beauty of a pastel sunset — in all of these we are struck dumb with awe by the majesty and variety of this good earth which is our home. And all of this calls beyond itself, speaking in a language, which our souls comprehend, of the One whose fiery imagination has sung all this into being. It awakens within us a desire to respond and participate; to allow the massive hymn of creativity to flow through us and out into the world in a sympathetic celebration of irrepressible life and joy. By opening ourselves to divine creative passion, we find that God-breathed spirit resonating within us and rendering harmonies.

To be human is to be creative. It is to take that which has been given and reshape it under the power of inspiration (literally, breathing) in such a way that it is even more beautiful and resplendent. In each soul there is a divine spark of creativity which has the potential to ignite and flame the whole of life. When allowed to burn unhindered, this blazing force can produce such results as to make God weep. One need only listen to the music of a Hildegaard von Bingen or a Mozart to understand what it is we are capable of. Naturally, not all of us are great composers or even artists in the technical sense of the word. But, in a broader sense, painting on the canvas of life with the soft brush of our individual talents, we are all involved in making a work of art. It can be enlightening to understand that life is not so much a chore to be accomplished as an invitation to artistry.

Every one of us is capable of transforming base materials into gold, once we give ourselves permission to do so. We all work with different materials, converting them into something which has been dreamed in the furnace of imagination. One person may take their experience of deep suffering and coin it into joyous empathy. Another might

begin with poverty and rework it into a warm generosity.
Yet another could start with silence and fashion it into poetry.
Or a little money could be used to enable a venture which
not only produces goods but also provides a source of
employment. The ways in which creativity is allowed to
operate are as varied as the people in which it burns. But
always that which springs from it is more beautiful and
complex than it was at the beginning of the process. And,
in each creative act, our souls have been allowed to speak,
bringing us deep contentment. The uniqueness which is ours
alone to give has come to expression.

Like so many other things of which we have
been speaking, the wellspring of creativity lies in the inner
life. We harbour the spark in our hearts, and part of the
responsibility of being human is to tend the ember until it
is fanned into a flame. Creativity is very simple in essence.
It might be expressed in an almost mathematical formula:
reality + imagination = creativity. It is in the chamber of the
imagination that the seemingly mundane is transformed into
something life-giving. Therefore it is important to nurture
and feed our imaginations on every possible occasion. Often
they are best encouraged through regular grazing on the
creative endeavours of others, whether the works of God in
nature, or the works of other artists in galleries, concert halls
and poetry collections. Once awakened, the imagination

begins its delicate interplay with the raw materials of life and makes something new from them.

 A small boy came to watch a sculptor at work. In a vast room, the artist was preparing to work on a huge slab of marble. For some hours, the sculptor walked round and round the stone, looking at it from every angle. Eventually he built some scaffolding around it, and began chipping away with hammer and chisel. The boy looked on, fascinated. Each day the boy would come back to watch what progress was being made. It was a long and slow process. But, gradually, the beginnings of a shape emerged from the labours. One day, for the first time, the boy thought he understood what it was that was being sculpted from the marble. He could hardly contain his excitement. Sure enough, as he returned over the next few days, it became clearer that what was being carved was a ferocious lion, crouched ready to pounce. As it was finished off, the boy marvelled at the lifelike strength and energy of the great beast, at times feeling a little anxious when left alone with it. The day came when the scaffolding was removed, and both the sculptor and the boy beheld the lion in all its majesty. 'It's lovely,' said the boy, 'but there's one thing I don't understand.' 'What's that?' asked the sculptor. 'Well,' puzzled the boy, 'how did you know that lion was in the stone when you started?' The sculptor laughed, and then considered the question. 'I knew the lion was in the stone,' he said, 'because I saw it first in my heart.'

The imagination is the womb of creativity. In it we sustain and protect foetal ideas, preparing them for their eventual journey into the world. During the period of gestation, our creative ventures are extremely vulnerable. They are particularly susceptible to criticism, which may cause them to wither and perish before ever experiencing life. We need to be careful about the people and environments we expose them to in these early stages. Many visions need a time in silence and darkness before they are ever articulated. There they gain strength and resilience, and begin to take on a life of their own. In the Christian story of creation, the Spirit hovers like a bird over the dark waters of chaos, preparing them for the call to being. It is a helpful image for considering our own creative processes.

There are a large number of opportunities in the space of a lifetime for expressing ourselves creatively. But always, buried deep within each soul, there is one thing that is uniquely ours to bring into the world, which no one else can replicate. If we fail to discover and incarnate that dream, then the rich symphony of life will be the poorer for it. No one else can tell us what our particular gift is, though others may help to provoke and draw it out of us. It is there, nonetheless, cocooned safely in our souls until the time of birth. So it is that in the flowering of the soul — when we reach that time of life when the true life emerges into view for us — some new responsibility may become apparent. We may find ourselves filled with a quiet longing which has previously been unknown to us. Sometimes this is a surprise to those who thought they knew us, as well as to ourselves. Such quiet promptings should not be ignored lightly. They are the birth pangs of the spirit.

If the imagination is the womb of creativity, then prayer is the amniotic fluid in which it is bathed. In prayer and meditation, we become still and wait expectantly. We empty ourselves, and listen for those fluttering wings on the waters of chaos which have been generated in the inner chambers. There may appear to be nothing happening. In fact it is the very absence of activity, thought, intention and desire which are the hallmarks of prayer. But what we are doing is creating space — space for our souls, space for God and space for the creative spark which glows in the dim vaults of imagination. Given these conditions, the spark will ignite just as surely as a seed sprouts when given soil, warmth and water. There is a force at work which is not of our own making, and yet without our cooperation it is unable to reach fulfilment. This is the mystery of incarnation — a process which touches all of us at some time in our journey.

Then there is the hard work of creation. For us it is not simply a matter of calling things into being and having them appear before us. We need to labour and craft in order to achieve that which we have glimpsed in our imaginations. That is an absolutely vital part of the process. Having seen something in our souls, we start working to bring the dream into some form of reality. The end to which we are labouring may at first seem vague and ill-defined. Only as we make progress towards it does it begin to become more distinct and recognisable. In our shaping and refining of the creative urge we pour something of ourselves into it, and so, in a way, this life's work becomes a child of ours. Art always has an element of divine inspiration within it, but the realisation is human. It is co-creation, one of the most satisfying vocations possible. We cannot separate ourselves from that which we create, and nor should we. The products of our imagination are intimately connected to us, and bear our image.

For the soul to flourish, we need to shake off the idea that somehow we are passive participants in a drama over which we have no control. We have been given the potential to not only shape our own lives, but to contribute to the entire canvas of the universe. To be a creator and artist is to know that your life has dignity and significance. Humanity has been honoured in the world by sharing in the possibility of creative transformation. With that honour comes responsibility not to fritter our talents away in a labyrinth of routine and convention. Rather, we must take whatever chances come to give voice to the imaginings of our hearts. We have been made to create, and in doing so we find something of the meaning of our existence.

DISAPPOINTMENT AND PAIN

Pain is a constant of human existence. It is a consequence of life; in fact numbness is one of the characteristics of death. Life cannot be tackled apart from the experience of pain and disappointment. Everybody hurts, and it is time we admitted that there are no means of navigating our destinies without suffering. Whether life would be conceivable without the dimension of pain is a moot point and an abstract discussion; certainly it would not be life of the sort we currently enjoy, with its full and genuine freedom. For most of us, the reality of suffering is not so much a metaphysical quandary as a harsh reality which must be confronted and processed for our own spiritual welfare. When we ask, 'Why is this happening to me?' we are not looking for explanations, but expressing protest and anguish.

Suffering is a great mystery, and the encounter with it is an unwelcome but necessary part of our journey. While we need to work ceaselessly to relieve the pain of others, the struggle with our own is not only unavoidable but contains lessons for us which can be learned no other way. It comes upon us in ways we cannot anticipate and would prefer to avoid. Indeed, the avoidance of pain has become a major preoccupation and a persistent source of spiritual sickness within our world. The mechanisms we use to either escape discomfort or dull our senses to reduce it are ultimately self-destructive. But the path to growth lies in moving ahead, encountering the fresh winds of pain and allowing them to blow through our lives at the appropriate time. No one ever made spiritual progress without traversing such territory. There are things to be learned in the travel through rugged terrain that can be discovered there alone.

In my earlier years I occasionally experienced such anguish of spirit that I thought it would be impossible to keep breathing through it. But I found to my astonishment that the human soul is incredibly resilient, and that the old cliché was true — that which doesn't kill us makes us stronger. At times I also thought that no one else in all of history had feelings quite like mine. And then, gradually, I noticed the eyes of people who had done a little living, and was introduced to a widespread community — the silent fellowship of suffering. A surprising feature struck me when I came across such folk: they seemed to me to be gentle and interesting people. Among them I didn't need to explain myself. And yet there was an unspoken communication which passed among us and assured us that we had each been to the dark side and returned.

In episodes of pain we find that all of our pretensions and social conventions, which form part of the mask we present to the world, are stripped away. The energy normally used to convince others that we are reasonable people is diverted to the simple task of survival. The inner chasm swallows any false projections, leaving us exposed. But it is precisely in such times of honesty that the issues and challenges of life are revealed in all their clarity. Suffering people are uncomplicated, with their protective illusions whittled away. Pain is a great purifier. Those who receive its embrace know that they are in raw contact with life and that, however chaotic their inner life, it is essentially true. The luxury of distraction is not available to them. The soul rises to the surface like a silver fish hooked by a wire barb. They have no choice but to be aware of their inner world, so intrusive is it on every other part of their lives.

The more we love, the more open we become to suffering. In love we are vulnerable, not just to our own hurt but to that of our beloved. I thought I knew what it was to suffer, and then I had children. My eldest daughter, a lovely gentle child, was raped at the age of eleven. She kept this secret from us until she was fifteen. The violation of her spirit was such that she found life too much for her to face unassisted. She became a morphine addict. Only those who have lived with addicts can know the devastation and ongoing chaos which ensues. In order to support her habit, she became a prostitute. I cannot begin to describe the pain involved with watching the life of someone you love dearly being destroyed before your eyes, and being powerless to prevent it. Suffice it to say that I became an intimate companion of agony. During each day the pain formed a deadening backdrop to everything else that happened. By night I lay awake, unable to sleep for the physically crushing weight of it all. I would gladly have traded my own death or suffering for that of my daughter, but that was not an option open to me.

I won't pretend that I didn't consider suicide as an option; a way of putting a full stop to the daily assault crippling my spirit. I'm not sure what held me back — perhaps a deep intuition that, for all its abhorrence, this path was the one I had been given to walk. My daughter certainly attempted suicide on frequent occasions. I lost count of the number of times we were summoned to the Accident and Emergency ward in the dead of night. She didn't succeed, often despite very serious intentions. The worst thing was that I sometimes secretly wished she would succeed, simply because it would put a stop to the hurt. I'm ashamed to admit it, but those in deep pain slip past convention and rationality. Death would have brought a finality and marker point to the suffering, rather than the continued open-ended bleeding which was my reality. Eventually the event which turned things around was one none of us could have foreseen.

My daughter's best friend at this stage was a fellow-addict and prostitute, a sixteen-year-old girl by the name of Sarah. One night, while in the detoxification unit of the hospital, she hanged herself. It provoked an obvious crisis, which could have pushed my daughter either way. As it happened, it prompted her towards the desire for life, and she decided to make a desperate attempt to escape the dark world that held her captive. She began a long and complicated journey out of addiction; a daily struggle against physical and spiritual cravings which demanded enormous willpower. It is not over yet, some three years later, and perhaps never will be. There have been relapses and disasters, each of them bringing a fresh onslaught of pain and failure. She is struggling towards the light and towards life, but the forces arrayed against her are many and powerful. She remains a beautiful gentle creative spirit, and whatever happens will take away nothing from the unique gift to us of her life.

I do not speak of these things easily, nor through some maudlin desire to display my private life in public.

Rather, I want to establish some credentials for being able to speak about pain, and perhaps to be able to hold out some realistic hope to others who are trapped in circumstances which seem unendurable. Suffering has hollowed me out and left me empty. In the initial stages of learning of my daughter's rape I wanted revenge. I wanted to find the man responsible and make him pay for what he had done. Over time I came to accept that, attractive as it may seem, it would not change the terrible reality with which I had to live. I reluctantly let go of my anger and felt it slip away. Any sense of understanding of what had happened was stripped away in the early days of grief, and has never returned. I did not look for explanations; nor could any of them have eased the pain. When well-meaning people offered them to me, I found myself growing impatient and irate. Neither words nor theories went any distance towards lessening the grim truth of my inner anguish.

It is a difficult task to speak of the learning which suffering brings, because to do so carries a subtle suggestion that the struggles we encounter have been laid upon us simply for our education. In my own case, I would have trouble in continuing to believe in the goodness of God if I thought the anguish of the past few years had been organised as a kind of endurance test. For the most part, suffering is pointless and demeaning; if none of us would willingly

impose it on our children or loved ones, we can trust that
God would be even more reticent than us. Nevertheless, life
is neither possible nor conceivable without disappointment
and pain — a reality which no doubt impacts on divine
experience as much as it does on ours. And, in the crucible of
harsh circumstances, those who are committed to the sacred
journey will learn much to assist them on their way.

What then are some of the lessons to be learned
in the furnace? Acceptance of others is one. Only those who
believe themselves to be strong and secure can feel self-
righteous about the failures of their acquaintances. When
pain begins its inevitable deconstruction, we discover that
any moral high ground we may have previously occupied
is excavated from under our feet. Whereas we might, in
happier times, have been tempted to exercise judgment on
others from our position of strength, we are now unwilling
to condemn any. Those who suffer greatly are explorers of
the continent of grace, not because of any great insight but
because their own anguish prevents them from expecting
too much from the people around them. The word 'humility'
shares a certain affinity with the word 'humus' or 'soil' —
in some ways it is a quality that results when all the
skyscrapers of our ego have been levelled to the earth.

There is one exception to this path of humiliation
and humility. When people refuse to accept suffering, and

instead make it a private source of rage and bitterness, then rather than offering kindness and grace they begin to strike out with all the deadly intent of poisonous snakes. Pain is like water; it must be allowed to flow or else it stagnates. To harbour pain and use it to fuel anger is to wreak havoc for the soul which enwombs it, and for everyone around. The progress of a soul in pain is demonstrated by the fruits: bitterness for those who hold onto their suffering in outraged resistance, and humility for those who go with the flow of it and find themselves washed up in new territory.

We spoke in an earlier chapter of patience and the difficulties of learning it. Suffering is the surest taskmaster when it comes to attaining this quality. Those who suffer learn endurance, because they have no choice. They learn to rise in the morning in pain, and go to their bed in pain. To their own amazement, they discover that is possible not only to go about the basics of life, but also to do the occasional creative or loving thing while carrying an enormous burden of hurt on their backs. In so doing — in their very perseverance — such wayfarers both attain and recognise a certain dignity of suffering. We are ennobled and made more human through our endurance of pain.

Most importantly, we learn what hope is. Not the cheap and easy hope which dreams of wealth and comfort, but the deep hope which is able to sustain life in appalling circumstances. To continue breathing in the face of insurmountable odds is an affirmation of the enduring value of life itself. Those who have passed through the fire and are able to come out the other side still speaking of love become living emblems of hope. They are able to extend realistic hope to others simply through their presence and the occasional word of encouragement. Their words are made trustworthy because of their qualifications of pain. By their survival and commitment, they give testimony to the goodness of life and the necessary perseverance of the soul in its onward journey.

REGRETS, I'VE HAD A FEW...

One of the features of mid-life is a sense of failure and diminished opportunity.

When we are young everything seems possible and the future limitless. We entertain dreams effortlessly, confident of our own ability to achieve them. But the mid-point of life is a time of sober reassessment. We often look back on those early dreams as being impossibly naive. They flew as high as we wanted them to fly, but seldom did they take account of such inconvenient forces as gravity. When we succeeded, we counted this as further evidence of our inevitable achievement and glorious future. When we failed, we refused to be cowed and counted the experience as a minor setback on the path to accomplishment. After all, there was plenty of time left…

But when we reach a certain point in our spiritual pilgrimage, usually coinciding with mid-life, we begin to do two things. One is that we look ahead, and catch sight of the looming prospect of the end of life. For the first time, future existence begins to have an outer boundary. There is a defined distance between the present and the end of our earthly journey, and therefore only a certain number of achievements which might punctuate that final sojourn. The other thing we do is to look back the way we have come. This too is disconcerting, and often results in a sense of disappointment. All those things we were going to do and become; where have they all gone? Why have our talents not quite been recognised in the way we hoped, nor our efforts rewarded? Why have we come to accept such compromises when we set out with such strong ideals?

So much is normal. The sense of disquiet and even depression is entirely typical of the mid-life transition. To know that is in itself sufficient to offer a little relief to those who become despondent and moribund. But what do we do with all those regrets — those failed visions, untasted dreams and unfulfilled intentions? How do we reassess our lives and remotivate ourselves to carry on into the future without being crippled by despair? Clearly there is a need to confront the reality of our lives and destinies, but to do it in a way which can enhance spiritual progress, rather than curtail it. It is a matter not only of surviving this stage of our journey, but of growing through it so that we emerge on the other side better equipped for the remaining adventures.

Regrets can be entirely disabling. Everyone who reaches the midway point in life has them, and it would be dishonest to claim otherwise. We look back on the panorama of our lives and become intensely conscious of opportunities which have been missed, decisions which have gone the wrong way and circumstances which have conspired against us. There are critical instances of the journey which we would like to be able to revisit, knowing what we now know. There may be relationships which we wish we'd fought a little harder to hang onto, or decisions we avoided and wish we could change in retrospect. But now the opportunity has gone. We sit silent, powerless and dumbfounded as we review our lives and begin to accept that what has slipped away from us is irretrievable.

It was in the midst of such ruminations some years ago that I wrote a poem which expressed something of my inner emptiness and sense of disappointment for the way my life had turned out. At the time of writing it I was, to all intents and purposes, contentedly ensconced in my career. But shortly afterwards I resigned, an outward expression of the inner readjustments which mid-life brought to me as an unsought gift.

I for an I

At ten past three
On a wet afternoon
I observed a man
Living my life.

He carried it off
With surprising ease,
Dispensing smiles
Like painkillers.

Between phone calls
He stared at the window
As if there were something
    dead
Fixed on the glass.

'Who are you?'
I asked him.
'I have come to relieve you,'
He said.

'Don't forget my commitments,'
I tendered,
Wanting to make myself
Useful.

But the imposter
Was already busy
Signing cheques
And making appointments.

Without further ado
I turned away,
Looking for a life
That fit.

Happily, I did manage to find 'a life that fit'. But not before a large amount of turmoil had changed me and those with whom my life was intimately interwoven.

While regrets might be unavoidable, they are also unproductive on their own. They focus attention on what has been lost, with little attention to what might be gained in the process. To suffer the loss of hopes and ideals can feel devastating, and for some people brings an effective end to their energy for the ongoing pilgrimage of life. If failure is the judgment applied to the past, then it is easily carried forward as a prognosis for the future. It becomes self-fulfilling. But such self-pity is neither necessary nor enabling. We may not have become the people we imagined ourselves to be. Perhaps our sense of disappointment is merely the encounter with the people that we actually are; and our earlier assessments of who we were and what we should be aiming at were conditioned by our youth and immaturity.

If this is so, then our regrets and discontent should be seen as merely the accompaniment to awakening. At an earlier stage of life the goals we had may well have been shaped by the desire for external benefits such as recognition, status or wealth. In the life of the soul, however, these are surprisingly fickle enticements. They sparkle but they do not endure. To regret that we have not attained them at mid-life is to become fixated on what is passing away rather than growing alert to that which is rising. For it is in this period of our lives that we make a major shift, and the deeper tasks of existence come into view. It is a period of significant readjustment, which has the potential to make life richer and more lovely than it ever has been.

 A certain woman set out to find wealth and beauty. She had heard the story of a place beyond the desert where the mountains were made of gold, and where there was a spring of perpetual youth. Anyone who bathed in that spring would have the effects of age reversed, and their beauty restored. She travelled long across the desert, at times losing confidence in her ability to reach the other side. But the mountains loomed in the distance, and she continually refreshed herself with the dream of what she would find when she got there. The days turned into weeks, and the weeks into months. The number of travellers she met on the path dwindled until she reached the edge of the desert on her own.

The woman made her way through steep river gorges up into the mountains. She had little idea of where she was going, apart from the rumours she had heard and the tug of her own vision. More fruitless weeks were spent exploring. And then one day she came over a ridge and discovered a small pool surrounded by golden rocks. She could hardly contain her

*joy at having discovered her goal. So excited was the woman
that she could not decide what to do first: whether to dig out
some of the gold or to bathe in the magical waters. But the
lure of the pool was too great, and she disrobed and stepped
into it.*

*As the waters closed over her, she held onto the
conviction that anyone who bathed here would have the
effects of age reversed. And immediately she could feel the
magical waters working their mysterious powers. Then it
seemed that she was waking up. She looked around and could
not see the pool. Instead she was back in her home town on
the other side of the desert. And she was a young woman,
dreaming of a place where it was rumoured there was instant
wealth and beauty…*

The coming of mid-life is an opportunity to realise
that it is not what we have lost or failed to achieve which is
important, but that our immature desires might have been
misplaced. The very worst experience is to have achieved
everything that youth held out to us as being important,
only to find it empty and unable to satisfy the deep longing
of our souls. Then the transition to new goals becomes truly
difficult, because we have so much to lose. So it is that mild
disappointments in the middle of life may actually provide
freedom and flexibility to reorder our lives, rather than

engender disillusionment. The last half of life, in which we travel towards the horizon of death, requires a new set of motivations and goals. Regrets are a potential quagmire which can bog us down and hamper the journey of the soul. When they are allowed to set up camp in our hearts, they become a means of holding onto something which needs to be released.

When I was young, a friend and I went to visit my sister and her husband. They lived in a rural area, and we grew to enjoy farm life. One day my friend and I were out walking in the fields early in the morning, and came across masses of mushrooms. The discovery made us greatly excited. Here was this food springing up from nowhere, and freely available. We hatched a plan. We would gather as many mushrooms as possible, and when we travelled back to the city the next day, we would sell them and be rich. We went home and collected plastic bags in which to gather them, and toiled for a few hours gathering our lucrative crop. Before long we had enough to fill a large suitcase.

My sister, who was planning tea for the night, asked if she might have a few of our mushrooms. I considered the great value of these delicacies, and told her that if she wanted some she would have to pay for them. Naturally enough she was reluctant to go along with this, and so declined the deal. I felt

a little bad about it, but the thought of my incipient wealth
comforted me. It took most of the next day to return home, and
so it wasn't until the next day that we prepared to hawk our
mushrooms. But, when I opened the suitcase, all of the precious
cargo were mouldy and inedible. All I had was a case of rotten
food.

In a similar way, dreams which are held onto for
too long can become putrid and a source of spiritual decay.
If they are intentions which should have been laid aside,
but instead have become a spur to deep regret, they have the
potential to poison our future progress. Regret easily slips
into resentment, and resentment breeds bitterness. Before
long we have become miserable people, unable to experience
joy ourselves and angry at those who do express it. There are
some people who leave a bedroom untouched after the death
of a loved one. It starts as a reminder, becomes a memorial,
and eventually is a tomb in which life and hope are frozen.
Regret can function in the same way if it is clutched to the
heart in protest. Better to acknowledge the pain and move
on, carrying forward little but the capacity to hope again and
to vest that hope in worthy ends.

Fortunately for us, the road of life leads on, no
matter how many wrong turns we may have made along
the way. Rather than looking back over our shoulders in

mourning, we do better to lift our eyes to the new horizon which continues to beckon us, and leave our regrets quietly by the side of the road.

LIES, DAMNED LIES

Some spiritual realities need to be mentioned only in passing, because to dwell on them is to feed that which should not be fed. Evil is one such. It is the reality which has no reality; a force which is only fuelled by undue attention. Unfortunately, pilgrims on the sacred journey need to be aware of it or else they may be consumed by it.

Call it what you will — evil, the dark side, malevolence, the demonic — there is a power at work within the realm of the spirit which is focused on violence and destruction. When it is least acknowledged and recognised, then evil becomes most dangerous in individuals and in communities. Ignorance or dismissal of this force is no defence against it. As pilgrims of the soul, we need to be aware of but not obsessed by evil.

At the heart of this dark power is the proclivity for deception. The essence of evil is to deceive, distort and confuse. It prospers by imitating that which is good and true, only to invade and colonise it with death. Some religious systems would deny the existence of evil, and in a way they are right. It is an illusion to the extent that it has no life in itself; it is entirely parasitic. But, for practical purposes, those who live and work for love in the world find need of the category of evil to make sense of their experience. Some sections of the Western community consider themselves very sophisticated and 'beyond' the concepts of good and evil. Unfortunately, their superior intellects do not seem to protect them from being servants to that which they deny the existence of. We need only mention concentration camps and nuclear weapons to be aware of what the 'highest' civilisations are capable of.

The association of evil with darkness in the popular imagination is based on the comparison with lack of visibility. During the day it is easy to see both landmarks and obstacles, but when the night comes it is very difficult to distinguish one from the other. That is a useful analogy for the way in which evil creates confusion wherever it spreads. Issues which were previously clear become mired in layers of subtlety until no one can be sure what is happening any more. And even when terrible things are being done, it is not at all certain how they occur or who is responsible. Indeed, lack of responsibility is one of the hallmarks of evil. There is an anonymous character to the cold force which actively diminishes life and beauty in a voracious appetite for destruction.

There is a long distance between wrongdoing and evil, and it is of no help to any of us to make a simple equation between them. We all at times act in bad ways, and the shadow side of our personality can be a healthy part of our complex identity. But in the continuous spectrum between bad and evil, there is some indeterminate region in which a boundary is crossed. Usually it is occasioned by repeated and unrepentant acts of deception. Sustained lying seems to create some sort of vulnerability to a deeper corruption. Psychologists speak of dissociation, a mechanism by which people are able to perform horrendous deeds and yet create enough psychic distance for themselves that they fail to feel any guilt or remorse. In my personal pilgrimage to Dachau concentration camp, the most chilling aspect for me was a letter from the camp doctor accompanying a gift of chocolate and thanking the commandant's wife for her hospitality. By day this same doctor performed unspeakable experiments on the prisoners.

Evil is comparatively rare in its strong form, in which it is sometimes referred to as 'demonic'. But, at various points on our journey, all of us feel its gravitational pull upon us and are tempted towards experimentation with it. There is a certain seductiveness in the lust, power and energy offered by evil. Many people succumb to 'playing' with the dark side. Some of them never recover. There is a terrible naivety abroad when it comes to the encounter with spiritual forces. Those who embark on the journey of the soul begin like children in a minefield, and commonly need a guide to help them through their early explorations.

On my nineteenth birthday, one of my friends gave me an LSD tablet. At the time I was something of an 'acid-head', trying to find the meaning of life through psychoactive drugs. I swallowed the small orange pill, and embarked on an unusually intense trip. At the peak of it, I found myself in a realm of cold remote darkness. There were voices calling to me. They encouraged me to step outside of my body and join them. It was fine out there, they assured me. Some of the voices I recognised as those of my friends. Why not? I thought. And yet there was some residual anxiety which made me hesitate before breaking my link with earthly existence.

While I was caught up in this dramatic 'hallucination', I had slipped into a coma. My friends were gathered around me, unsure what to do. They didn't want to call an ambulance because there were illicit drugs involved. But they were concerned about my lack of breathing, and worried that I might die if left unattended. One friend, with no faith of his own, knelt beside me praying. Eventually I recovered. We discovered later

that the LSD had been cut with strychnine and other
substances. The voices which called to me were real enough,
and there may have been real consequences if I had responded.

The perverse nature of evil is that sometimes the fear of it can create the very conditions in which it thrives. There is nothing like a community of people who locate evil in some other group to produce the perfect incubator for hatred and prejudice. Therefore one of the keys to disarming the effects of it is to confront evil first in one's own spirit, and so be equipped to recognise and respond to it in other settings. For this to happen demands that we meet and embrace what Jung has described as the shadow side of our beings. It is not generally until mid-life that we even begin to become aware of this dark companion, let alone prepare ourselves for encounter with it. Some people, who do not take the time or trouble to reflect on their journey, may never get to the point of recognition of their shadow side. We who examine our souls, however, will scarcely be able to avoid it when the right time has come.

In crude terms, the shadow is formed by the repression of those parts of our personalities that are unacceptable either to our own ideals about who we are, or else to family and societal conventions. Because the latter forces are dominant in early development, there are large parts of the self that are censored and suppressed. They still have influence over us, but are experienced as dark and distant forces which come upon us. It is in the middle period of our lives that we are able to evaluate and perhaps stand apart from societal convention, and so begin the process of reclaiming those aspects of personhood which have been consigned to the garbage. In this embrace of our own darkness, we find reconciliation, wholeness and maturity. We may also better recognise our own susceptibility to all the perversity of which humanity is capable. Spiritual and emotional maturity demands awareness of the evil which is not only around us but within us.

It is in denial that real troubles start. When we begin not only to try to convince others, but also to believe for ourselves that there is nothing bad within us, then we are flirting with real danger. In self-deception genuine evil may gain a foothold, festering in hidden darkness until an opportunity presents itself to erupt in a seething force which sweeps all before it. Strangely enough, many religious systems function in an unhelpful way by forcing the shadow side of human life underground, where it does much more damage than if acknowledged openly. Deception and concealment are the allies of evil, while honesty, humanity and humour are its enemies. In the ancient biblical story of temptation, it is the fruit from the tree of knowledge of good and evil which is said to bestow divine spiritual power.

To preserve ourselves from evil, and to help cleanse it from the world, it is necessary that we become adept at telling the truth. This sounds rather simple, but in reality is one of the hardest things on earth to achieve. In order to tell the truth, we must first be prepared to listen to it, to hear things about ourselves which we might prefer not to. We need to be willing to lay aside all of our defence mechanisms and ruses by which we convince ourselves and others that we're really very nice people. We have to be sufficiently in tune with our souls to know what it is that's happening on the inside of us. We need to know when to speak and when to keep silent. We must distinguish between words of healing and words of condemnation. And all of this is only the beginning of honesty. It demands of us that we be introspective people, that we listen carefully and discriminatingly for the whispers of the spirit which will guide us.

The effort is worth it. When we learn to speak the truth, it becomes easier to live as honest people — that is to say, as people in whom word and deed are consistent. To speak the truth is not to become popular. It is to be often misunderstood and sometimes regarded as subversive. Honesty produces conflict, because in a world where delusion is preferred it represents treason. But once we have learned to trust the inner voice, and taken care to know ourselves, then we have nothing to fear from all the forces arrayed against us. Deceit and lies can never overcome truth, however much damage they may appear to cause in the short term. Ingrained dishonesty and the evil it produces are ultimately self-defeating.

In tackling evil, there is a paradoxical feature which is best learned early. Whenever impure motives are involved in attacking evil, it grows stronger rather than weaker. The best strategy is in fact the oblique one: the active non-violent confrontation which speaks the truth in the face of lies and bears whatever consequences might result. Two of the best examples of this in recent history are provided by Mahatma Gandhi and Martin Luther King, Jr, both of whom gave their lives in the cause of love. Each of these men drew on spiritual forces to sustain them in resisting evil without adopting its tactics. Because of that, their legacy for change lives on, and they remain as inspirational models. That which they learned in the silent chambers of their souls stood them in good stead when it came to the defeat of the powerful and malevolent powers arrayed against them.

It is never a good idea to set out on a crusade to vanquish evil, either from ourselves or from society at large. By campaigning against it, we simply draw attention to that which has no life in itself. Far better to make love our goal, and to refine our own love so that it becomes a source of hope and healing in a confused world. Evil has no weapons against love, even though at times it seems to have eradicated it. When the light comes on, the shadows flee, and we understand that they were mere phantoms. When the light of God dawns within us, there is no room for darkness and we are bathed in life-giving radiance. Let us not fall into the mistake of comparing the absence of light to light itself, as if they were somehow equivalent in power and importance. Only the light will endure, and the darkness will flee.

MONEY FOR NOTHING

Some people consider that money has little to do with the life of the soul, and that the material and spiritual should be kept separate from each other. It is hard to know how that would be possible in the world in which we now live. Money is a universal symbol which governs our relationship to work, possessions, lifestyle and aspirations — all of which are of spiritual significance. What we do with our money will be expressive of our inner life. Correspondingly, the journey and progress of the soul will change our relationship to and handling of money. Whether we like it our not, the two spheres of human experience are closely related and intersect at too many points for them to be regarded in isolation from each other.

Having established this, it must be admitted that there can be wide divergences in attitudes to life, dependent on whether it is money or soul which is dominant in setting priorities. When the spiritual life is foremost, and we focus on the inner journey, then money and possessions are viewed as almost incidental to that pilgrimage. Conversely, when financial issues occupy the centre of our attention, it is the spiritual which tends to be regarded as peripheral. The amount of resources which any individual has at their discretion is almost insignificant in comparison to the attitude held towards them. It is as possible for a poor person to live a generous and rich life as it is for a rich person to live a selfish and miserable life. What is important is that which lies in the heart.

We live in a culture which values commerce over faith, and regards it as self-evident that the pursuit of financial reward is a sufficient goal in itself. We also live in a culture in which people find themselves lonely, unsatisfied, empty and exhausted. It is worthy of consideration whether there might be some connection between these two conditions. To make of money a goal for life is to thirst for something which can never satisfy. Temporal goods can never fulfil a dislocation that is essentially spiritual. The more our society is hell-bent on evaluating people and life in purely economic categories, the more it will resemble not so much a community as a cattle market. The lack of balance between money and soul is wreaking havoc in the West, producing successful economies and soulless societies. Little wonder that suicide and drug abuse are widespread and endemic.

To take the sacred journey seriously is to put money in its proper place as a servant of the quest for fulfilment, rather than as director of it. Many years ago, Jesus told his followers not to be mindful of possessions. Rather, he said, fix your attention on the realm of God and its demands and all of the other things will be added to you. Here we have a very basic spiritual principle. When you give attention to the inner life, the outward structure of life begins to take care of itself. When it is neglected, then no amount of effort and hard work can achieve a harmonious state of existence. Some people work every hour that is available to them, driven by their quest to accumulate more and more. But they find no enjoyment in the money they collect, because they haven't given space for the cultivation of joy. Others spend regular time in prayer and silence, and glow with contentment even in the midst of very simple pleasures, because the source of their happiness is not determined by wealth.

On the face of it, money seems to be a fixed symbol — 'hard currency'. It represents a carefully defined amount of buying power, and the amount one has or doesn't have determines what options are open. As long as money is regarded in this way, it becomes a self-authenticating truth. It will be a static and dead resource, capable of a certain amount of manipulation, but little more. But we pilgrims of the soul discover a deeper and more mysterious character to money. When filtered through the life of the spirit, it develops a fluid and very flexible quality. No longer is it limited by the rules and confines of what can be calculated, but it seems to develop an almost independent life.

A man who was down on his luck received a chequebook in the mail. There was nothing to say who it was from, but the cheques had his name printed on them. For a while he consigned it to the drawer, assuming it was a mistake, and not wishing to commit fraud. Shortly afterwards he received a statement which showed a balance of five pounds. This was not much to get excited about, but he went out and spent it on a treat anyway. But, as times got tougher, the temptation of the chequebook grew too much. He went on a spending spree, writing cheques for hundreds of pounds. When the statement arrived the next month, he was dreading opening it. But, to his amazement, there was a deposit recorded which restored the balance to five pounds.

Over time he began to understand how it worked. However much he spent each month, there was always a deposit to make the balance stand at five pounds. It began to change the way the man lived. He became more generous and expansive. He spent less and less on himself, and more on others, so conscious was he of the generosity of his mysterious benefactor.

One day he learned that a friend of his was down on his luck and in need of money. He considered how he might help, and then hit on a plan. He arranged for a chequebook to be delivered anonymously to his friend, with a balance of five pounds. Somewhere, it seemed, he heard the sound of laughter drifting on the breeze.

While we may not receive a magic chequebook in the mail, it is possible to experience the strange elasticity of money when it is used as an accompaniment to the spiritual life. Even though we may be on fixed incomes, at those junctures of life when it is important for us to encounter a new experience for the enrichment of our souls, somehow there is money available for us to do so. We find ourselves surrounded by generous people who are willing to give of their excess, and their generosity begins to influence us. We become less guarded about our money and possessions, and more willing to use and share them for the benefit of others. All of this sounds very strange to the ears of a financial planner — perhaps even irresponsible. But to those who follow the sacred journey, it is simply a different way of regarding money which is more in keeping with our spiritual experience.

Another teaching of Jesus was that wherever our most precious things are, there our hearts will be also.

Whatever it is that we value most in life, that will be what captures and holds our inner aspirations. If it is material possessions, then we will be consumed by pursuit of them. They will be the goals towards which we strive, and the things which provide meaning for us. Often people who seek such rewards gain them, and fill their lives with innumerable belongings. These bring them a certain amount of satisfaction, and the feeling of having arrived. But there may also come an associated fear of death. Nothing is more certain than that all their accumulations will be stripped away by death, and so it is regarded as an enemy. There is, however, another type of treasure which might more suitably occupy our imaginations: spiritual wealth. This is a lasting resource which doesn't need insurance, retains its value and can never be taken away from its owner.

The treasure of the soul is more intangible but nonetheless real, and certainly more enduring than its physical counterpart. The cultivation of such assets as humility, compassion, patience, mercy, peace, hospitality and love will prepare us well for the ongoing life of the spirit. Access to such resources is entirely equitable, and the good news is they don't attract tax! They are completely portable, embedded as they are in the soul. When this kind of wealth becomes our motivation, there comes a glorious sense of freedom and detachment. Money may come and go, careers may wax and wane, fame may grow or diminish, but the real treasure of life will be safe and available at all times and in all places. Not even death can rob of us of these investments in spiritual currency.

When the prophet criticised the king, he sent his army to silence her. At first they removed her children, conscripting her sons into the army and her daughters into the royal household. But the prophet did not keep silence. When the army came again, they set her house alight and burned it to the ground. But the prophet did not keep silence. Next they went out into her fields and slaughtered all her stock and burned her crops. But the prophet did not keep silence. Eventually they took her into captivity, stripped her naked and incarcerated her in a small dark cell. But the prophet did not keep silence. She laughed at them. 'You have taken away everything, but you have taken nothing from me,' she told them. So they killed her. But the prophet did not keep silence. Her word is still heard today, long after the king is dead.

Once money has ceased to be the measure of all things, the world begins to look very different. The importance of people is not so easily evaluated by what can be seen. Neither the presence nor the absence of wealth are much of an indicator as to the wisdom or significance of those we meet. We need to become alert and attentive to people, listening beneath the surface fabric of their lives to hear the word they may have to speak to us. For ourselves, there comes a disconnection between the outward signs of material well-being and the inner life of the soul. We may be quite wealthy at some times and quite poor at others. Neither condition is necessarily an indicator of where we are on the journey of the spirit. The wise person will learn to be content with either poverty or wealth, recognising that these are temporary states which may be relevant to a particular stage of our pilgrimage.

The more material resources that are at our disposal, however, the more difficult it becomes to remain focused on the road we are called to follow. Much wealth brings many distractions, and to live well in its presence may require greater spiritual discipline than in humbler circumstances. It is easier to be generous with a little, when you don't have much to lose, than it is to be generous with a lot. Even so, wealth should not be despised, but rather recognised as demanding more responsibility from those who have it available. Often in mid-life people discover that they have greater disposable resources than they may have had at an earlier stage of life, and so there needs to be conscious attention given to the way in which money is used. Our goal should always be to retain wealth as a servant rather than as a master, and we must take care to keep it in this position.

It is better to look into the eyes of a person rather than into their wallet when trying to estimate their worth. Money is capable of changing the outside of the person, making them appear more beautiful, urbane and fashionable. But it can do nothing in and of itself to change what is in the heart, where the real seat of life lies. What is on the inside will be shaped by the life of the soul — a glorious existence to which money has little to contribute.

THE LAST LEAVING

Every journey must have an end, even if the end is sometimes the beginning. The end to which we are all travelling on earth is that of our death. This is the moment of truth and transition for us — all we are and all we have done becomes manifest. All of our living up until this point is leading us towards that unavoidable moment: our last leaving. The years of practice at letting go and holding life lightly are brought to the test when we must release that which has been absolutely fundamental to us — life itself. In the confrontation with death, every issue of spiritual existence becomes focused and intensified. Each of us faces it on our own, no matter how many people we may be surrounded with, and we must find our own way of making peace with its challenge. Death brings honesty to humanity, and has a way of sifting people to reveal what is in them.

We should not be fearful of it. Fear is a function of that which is unknown, and most who are spiritually attuned will have made acquaintance with the prospect of death long before it appears on the horizon. Death is not only natural, it can have a certain beauty about it. Both births and deaths are significant human experiences, and those who have been present during either will have become aware of their mystical quality. What creates the sense of fear and abhorrence about death is not so much the event itself, as the anticipated loss it will bring. Certainly it brings an abandonment of much that has been familiar: people we love, places of significance to us, life itself. If we have not learned the lesson of relinquishment, then we will fight against the process of dying and have a hard time of it. But for many of us, it comes as the anticipated graduation of a lifetime of learning.

I don't pretend to have any intimate knowledge of what lies on the other side of death. Those who do are usually fools or charlatans. All I know is what my soul whispers of, and that is that death is not an ending. Love is enduring, and able to overcome all obstacles — even that of death. This life of the spirit we have begun to sample cannot be extinguished through the demise of our bodies. We have hints already of the life to come. Intimations only — but sufficient to give us encouragement for hope beyond the grave. Even though we may not know the geography of that land beyond the last river, we know enough to be confident that there will one day be the opportunity to explore it for ourselves. For the present, our attention must be on preparing to successfully cross the border.

It is our final goodbye, and we should make as good a job of it as possible. One of the preparations we can make is that of keeping short accounts. It is not very practical to wait until the last weeks of our lives to make reconciliation with those from whom we are estranged. Not only will it become forced, if even possible, but we will have missed out on the joy of healed relationships which we might have carried as an abiding memory with us. The end of the journey brings many things into perspective, and perhaps in the knowledge of life's brevity we may begin to regard some things differently. Disputes which seemed important at the time appear almost trivial, while qualities such as friendship begin to assume greater importance. Under the shadow of impending death, forgiveness does not seem such a difficult burden to offer.

We also need to begin the process of loosening our hold on life, long before the final release comes. It is not necessary to withdraw from involvement in life, but rather to unclench our grip upon it. Every act of relinquishment is a preparation for it — we release those things we love and take the risk of losing them. Like everything else, the act of letting go requires practice if it is to be done well. If we have prepared ourselves, we will not struggle against death but surrender to it with peace and equanimity. It will be the last great adventure of our earthly existence, in which we rely upon the goodness of God and freely plunge into the unknown. The confidence to do so is not found in the last hour of life, but slowly established over many years.

Just recently my wife became aware that the raising of our children had made her rather more cautious than she had been previously. She found herself afraid of taking risks, whether on her own behalf or that of others. Watching children play became difficult for her, as she was anxious that they might hurt themselves. Realising that she needed to break this pattern before it took hold, she determined to do something about it. Even though she was scared of heights, she decided that she would undertake a tandem paraglide from the top of a mountain. When the time came, she had to face the prospect of running off the side of a steep hill into nothingness. She was terrified, but she did it. When the flight was over, and she landed on solid ground again, she was glowing with satisfaction. She had faced her fears and overcome them. And, in a way, she had contributed to her preparations for the end of life.

The presence of God becomes an important ingredient in making the transition which death represents. Again, deathbed conversions may be possible and meaningful.

But how much better and more satisfying to have come to know and love God over the course of our lives, rather than waiting to the end and reaching out in desperation? When we know and are known by God, then we have the constant assurance of companionship. In all the many adventures which constitute our path through life, we have already learned that there is One who watches us and walks beside us. Along the way we have discovered that it is safe to let go of things, as long as we put our trust in God. When it comes at last to our death, we know we are not consigning ourselves into oblivion, but into the waiting arms of God.

 A man went looking for the meaning of life. He passed through forests and over mountains and across seas. He talked to people along the way. All the time he was looking and listening, desperate for a clue to the deepest puzzle. Sometimes he thought he was onto it. He would follow up hints of mystery and words of wonder with mounting excitement and anticipation. But always he was disappointed. The promise of meaning would dissolve like wood smoke in the air. Many of the people he trusted turned out to be tricksters or merchants. In sadness he finally accepted that there was no meaning to life at all. The man took himself to the middle of a great bridge spanning a river gorge, intending to jump into the chasm. He couldn't even think of any message to leave. So he simply jumped. Instead of

being smashed on the rocks below, he found himself caught in
a pair of arms strong enough to break his fall. 'Who are you?'
asked the man of his catcher. 'I'm the one who's been looking
for you,' came the reply.

The sadness in death is for those who are left behind, rather than those who are leaving. For the ones making the crossing, it can be a welcome homecoming after a long and testing journey. We are arriving in a place where we are known and loved, and where some of the limitations of earthly life may be overcome. In all of our pilgrimages we have been heading towards this destination and preparing ourselves for it. Finally we are reaching the end of the road, and there comes a sense of deep satisfaction that we have made it this far. The ones we leave behind we know are watched over by the same God who has beckoned us along the way, and so we can with sure hope cease our own strivings and relax into death.

Anything dying takes from us probably wasn't worth hanging onto anyway. And everything we are able to take with us is the fruit of our life's dedication to the spirit. In this sense, the end of life makes transparent the entirety of what has been contained by that life. Death is inevitable honesty, which may be why some people seek to avoid it so diligently. The attitude we bring to our dying is influenced by whether our attention is captured by that which lies over our shoulders and which we are leaving behind, or else by that which lies in front of us and beckons us from across the border. To look back is to fear loss and indulge ourselves in regret; to look forward is to embrace hope and surge on towards that for which we have been made. The habits of a lifetime may decide which direction engages our final gaze.

 Consider the chrysalis. It is the tomb of the caterpillar — a white shroud of death which marks the end of life as it has been known. As the caterpillar is encased by the spidery weave, it suffers an inevitable death to all that has come before. The experience is one of numbness and dissolution. Who could explain to the earthbound caterpillar what this process is about? How can the butterfly speak to the chrysalis of the life that is to come? And yet all of that beauty and grace of the butterfly, all of that majestic ability to fly and flutter, all of that is already contained in the potential of the caterpillar. All that stands between it and a glorious transformation is the white tomb, and the willingness to surrender life as it has been known.

We should not be dismayed by the limitations of our present existence. We cannot possibly envisage the life for which we are being prepared, and nor should we begin to try. It is the tasks and challenges of the immediate situation which consume, as they should. The best method of preparing for death and what lies beyond it is simply to commit ourselves wholeheartedly to the spiritual growth available in the moment. This is the mechanism by which our souls are being transformed. The day will come when they will burst forth and be unfurled in a blaze of glory, and we will marvel at what has happened within us. But that experience lies beyond the end of the path, and is not to be anticipated before its time. It is enough to rest in the sure knowledge that it will come, and to continue to live as those who have no need to fear death.

The remainder of the path stretches out towards the horizon. We have begun to register that there is a horizon to our journey, and to consider it seriously enough to prepare ourselves. It is not a journey we make alone, and yet each of us must take responsibility for our unique decisions and the directions they lead us in. We are following the greatest path of all — the pilgrimage of the soul. There is a light which shines upon our feet as we walk, and it is the light of God. With grace and a fair wind, we will reach the destination to which we are being called. Life is so much more than is apparent from the surface of it, and we have hardly begun to plumb its depths. It is a sacred journey, from birth to death. Godspeed as you go.

Endnotes

1. T.S. Eliot, 'The Love Song of J. Alfred Prufrock', *Selected Poems: T.S. Eliot*, London: Faber and Faber, 1961, p. 14.

2. C.G. Jung, *The Collected Works*, R.F.C. Jull, trans. Bollingen series XX, Princeton, NJ: Princeton University Press, 2nd ed., 1969, vol. 8, 'The Structures and Dynamic of the Psyche', par. 784, pp. 398–99.

3. Oliver Sacks, *The Man Who Mistook His Wife for a Hat*, Picador, 1985, p. 28.

4. Robert Frost, 'The Road Not Taken', *The Poetry of Robert Frost*, ed. Edward Connery Lathem, Jonathan Cape. Reproduced by permission of the Estate of Robert Frost.

5. Thomas Merton, *Thoughts in Solitude*, New York: Image Books, 1958, p. 81.

6. William Shakespeare, *The Merchant of Venice*, Act 4, Sc. 1, 1.

7. Kahlil Gibran, *The Prophet*, Oxford: Oneworld Publications (originally published in 1928).

Some stories are loosely based on the originals: p. 12 is based on a story by Paulo Coelho in *The Alchemist*; p. 22 is based on a story by James K. Baxter in *Jerusalem Daybook*; p. 86 is based on a story by Anthony de Mello in *The Song of the Bird*; p. 110 is based on a story by Anthony de Mello in *The Prayer of the Frog*; p. 116 is based on a story by William Bausch in *Storytelling: Imagination and Faith*; p. 140 is based on an Anthony de Mello story in *The Song of the Bird*; p. 174 is based on a story by Henri Nouwen.